SYSTEMS THINKING
FOR
HARASSED MANAGERS

Other titles in the
Systemic Thinking and Practice Series
edited by David Campbell and Ros Draper
published and distributed by Karnac

Asen, E., Dawson N. & McHugh B. *Multiple Family Therapy: The Marlborough Model and its Wider Applications*
Bentovim, A. *Trauma-Organized Systems: Physical and Sexual Abuse in Families*
Boscolo, L. & Bertrando, P. *Systemic Therapy with Individuals*
Burck, C. & Daniel, G. *Gender and Family Therapy*
Campbell, D., Draper, R. & Huffington, C. *Second Thoughts on the Theory and Practice of the Milan Approach to Family Therapy*
Campbell, D., Draper, R. & Huffington, C. *Teaching Systemic Thinking*
Campbell, D. & Mason, B. (Eds) *Perspectives on Supervision*
Cecchin, G, Lane, G. & Ray, W.A. *The Cybernetics of Prejudices in the Practice of Psychotherapy*
Cecchin, G., Lane, G. & Ray, W.A. *Irreverence: A Strategy for Therapists' Survival*
Dallos, R. *Interacting Stories: Narratives, Family Beliefs and Therapy*
Draper, R., Gower, M. & Huffington, C. *Teaching Family Therapy*
Farmer, C. *Psychodrama and Systemic Therapy*
Flaskas, C. & Perlesz, A. (Eds) *The Therapeutic Relationship in Systemic Therapy*
Fredman, G. *Death Talk: Conversations with Children and Families*
Hildebrand, J. *Bridging the Gap: A Training Module in Personal and Professional Development*
Hoffman, L. *Exchanging Voices: A Collaborative Approach to Family Therapy*
Johnsen, A., Sundet, R. & Torsteinsson, V.W. *Self in Relationships: Perspectives on Family Therapy from Developmental Psychology*
Jones, E. *Working with Adult Survivors of Child Sexual Abuse*
Jones, E. & Asen, E. *Systemic Couple Therapy and Depression*
Krause, I.-B. *Culture and System in Family Therapy*
Mason, B. & Sawyerr, A. (Eds) *Exploring the Unsaid: Creativity, Risks and Dilemmas in Working Cross-Culturally*
Robinson, M *Divorce as Family Transition*
Smith, G. *Systemic Approaches to Training in Child Protection*
Wilson, J. *Child-Focused Practice: A Collaborative Systemic Approach*

Work with Organisations

Campbell, D. *Learning Consultation: A Systemic Framework*
Campbell, D. *The Socially Constructed Organization*
Campbell, D., Coldicott, T. & Kinsella, K. *Systemic Work with Organizations: A New Model for Managers and Change Agents*
Campbell, D, Draper, R. & Huffington, C *A Systemic Approach to Consultation*
Cooklin, A. (Ed) *Changing Organizations: Clinicians as Agents of Change*
Haslebo, G. & Nielsen, K.S. *Systems and Meaning: Consulting in Organizations*
Huffington, C. & Brunning, H. (Eds) *Internal Consultancy in the Public Sector: Case Studies*
Huffington, C., Cole, C., Brunning, H. *A Manual of Organizational Development: The Psychology of Change*

Credit Card orders, Tel: + 44 (0)20 8969 4454; Fax: + 44 (0)20 8969 5585
Email: shop@karnacbooks.com

SYSTEMS THINKING
FOR
HARASSED MANAGERS

Nano McCaughan & Barry Palmer

Forewords by
Charles Hampden-Turner
Ian Sparks

Systemic Thinking and Practice Series
Work with Organizations

Series Editors
David Campbell & Ros Draper

London
K ARNAC BOOKS

First published in 1994 by
H. Karnac (Books) Ltd.
6 Pembroke Buildings
London NW10 6RE

Reprinted 2004

British Library Cataloguing in Publication Data
A C.I.P. for this book is available from the British Library

ISBN: 1 85575 055 4
www.karnacbooks.com

Printed & bound by Antony Rowe Ltd, Eastbourne

ACKNOWLEDGEMENTS

We would like to thank the managers of The Children's Society, who have sponsored and supported our recent courses; and the managers of the London Borough of Croydon Social Services Department, who supported the earlier courses.

We would also like to thank all the managers who have worked with us over the last eight years and have generously shared their problems and their insights with us and with each other.

And we would like to thank Jane Aaron for her helpful comments on drafts of chapters one, two, and six, and Oula Jones for generously agreeing to compile the index.

CONTENTS

EDITORS' FOREWORD

Fortunately for our field, Nano McCaughan and Barry Palmer have always been open to and interested in new ideas. Through experience of the group relations conferences organized by the Tavistock and Grubb Institutes, they became interested in the dynamics of organizational life, and in the early 1980s they began running their own workshops. They then became curious to know more about a new development known as systemic thinking. Since then they have been busily applying their ideas to the much neglected field of management development. Through years of managers' seminars they have now distilled the field of systemic thinking to key concepts and practices that have proven helpful to managers through the test of time.

Over the years we have been stimulated by discussions with them about their work and challenged to think of ways managers' dilemmas can be alleviated; now, in this volume, McCaughan and Palmer present their ideas and the result of many years' experience. The book demonstrates a synthesis of ideas and skills, both from the authors' own work and also from the wider field of consultancy; for example, they incorporate the work of Senge and Hampden-Turner.

Systemic ideas are carefully explained and contextualized; the usefulness of these ideas, both for managers and consultants, is then illustrated with "real-life" case studies. The book is very "grounded" in real, day-to-day, garden-variety problems that managers are facing in the 1990s. For readers interested in McCaughan and Palmer's method of teaching these new approaches, there is a concise description of their seminars in an appendix. We think the reader will learn from the process of reading this book, as well as from its content. It is a "say so" book in which the authors say what they do and do what they say.

David Campbell
Ros Draper

London
January 1994

FOREWORD

Charles Hampden-Turner

The Judge Institute of Management Studies,
University of Cambridge

NEW PARADIGMS FOR OLD

I have been asked to introduce this fascinating volume by Nano McCaughan and Barry Palmer. I gladly do so. We cannot have too much of this kind of writing. Few scholars genuinely understand systems thinking. Partial insights abound, but then "common sense" is reimposed and the significance lost. Such partial insights often do more harm than good. The insight that the world of living systems is recursive is too often regarded as something that afflicts everyone but the investigator. The commonest reaction is "stop the world, I want to get off". The consultant-cum-researcher looks down on the merry-go-round and like the Pharisee thanks the Lord that he is not as other men are. I call this the "potter's wheel" approach to cybernetics. What I seek to shape unilaterally is not on an assembly line but on a wheel, and to some extent the wheel's momentum will influence what I shape. This represents only a small improvement on scientism-as-usual, since others are still regarded as "clay between my hands". This book is one of the few to realize that we are *all* chasing our tails, all rotating endlessly. The consultant no less than the client is in the same vortex. We can come to grasp the power of the vortex but cannot gainsay its power over us. As Gregory Bateson points out, the first step in the cure of alcoholism by Alcoholics Anonymous is to acknowledge a power greater than yourself (see his seminal essay in *Steps to an Ecology of Mind*, 1972, pp. 309ff).

If I have any reservations about this book, it is that the scope for the application of systems theory is too circumscribed. There are ways of thinking, we are told, that will help harassed managers in otherwise intractable situations. A number of "soft" problems are not technical but systemic.

Quite so . . . but very few problems faced by our society do *not* in some degree involve living systems. And it is here that cause-and-effect calculations are not simply ineffective but *catastrophic*, in the original sense of Greek tragic drama. The word "catastrophe" means literally a "sudden downturn" in the fortunes of the hero. He acts tyrannically to "cause" something to happen, yet exactly the opposite results. The insight is over twenty centuries old and *still* we have not grasped it! Forgive my impatience.

What has long hidden our failure from us is the habit of subordination. Workers never *did* believe they were "hands", "factors", or "commodities", but pressured into behaving like machines they gave passable imitations; civil servants never *did* believe they were "servants", mere means to the ends decided by a sovereign parliament, but they went along with the prevailing myth. We see the joke when we watch *Yes Minister*, in which the "servant" ties the "master" in knots.

What is now rubbing our noses in the failure of the Newtonian paradigm is the end of subordination. In a society where the media sell irreverence and even royalty are lampooned, people are less and less willing to be billiard balls to someone who "calls the shots".

The present government has managed to get a few more years out of the old paradigm by visiting the consequences of our declining powers upon the poor and weak. Labour relations are said to have improved when workers obey rather than lose their jobs. Government workers obey lest the next cut cuts them. But all of this is made possible only by the economy's mounting crisis. What is wrong is not that people do not obey but that we expect them to obey. We pull levers and complain that the machine is broken. But it never was a machine . . . We should have listened in the days when people still had the courage to rebel. They were trying to tell us something.

Since the authors quote so liberally from *Alice in Wonderland*, may I remind them of Bateson's favourite part? This was the croquet game in which Alice tried to use a flamingo, live hedgehogs, and men bending over, as if they were a mallet, balls, and hoops. The flamingo turning its head to look at Alice as she tries to use it to hit the hedgehog, which has crawled off, is a wonderfully absurdist example of what happens when you pretend that living systems are but dead implements of your purposes.

We came close to genocide during the Cold War in attempting to "deter" the enemy, who is now known to have been more desperate than malevolent, more haunted by past suffering than minded to enslave the world. As for "wars" on drugs, prostitution, and alcohol, the authors reveal all of these to have the "rationality" of Wonderland croquet. All attempts to cause others to behave as if they were physical objects are doomed from the outset. The "deterrence" of criminals merely endorses the logic by which they themselves operate. Their methods, although turned against them, are vindicated by those in authority.

An example of how pristine logic comes unstuck is found in the welfare system. In order that the tax-payers' money not be wasted on the ineligible, claimants are carefully screened to make sure they are totally abject and certifiably helpless. Any hint of personal initiative, sources of emotional or financial support, undisclosed savings, or viable job prospects causes an angry furrowing of official brows. How *dare* you be anything more than desperate?

But at the same time the job-seeker is expected to show quite another face to would-be employers. She or he must personify initiative, skill, resources, contacts, confidence. But because employers are trying to maximize shareholders' returns, they will typically offer only casual or part-time labour to the previously unemployed. However well you work, your employer can save on social security and other fringe benefits by substituting another casual labourer in your place. You must then reapply for welfare, a time-consuming process in which you are once again at risk of being insufficiently abject to qualify.

Several million Britons are now trapped in this no-man's-land of insufficient competence and insufficient incompetence, shuttled to and fro between incompatible definitions of "eligibility", victims of the classical double-bind. In this trap, taxation is 100%, or even higher, since the time spent reapplying for welfare is seldom covered by welfare payments.

The irony is that the thinking of the welfare system and of the employment system are both immaculately rational. Yet *between* these logics real people are torn asunder by the resulting incompatibilities. Those who find themselves the targets of reasonable men are trapped in unreason. That some resort to fraud is hardly surprising, however regrettable. Many more live in desperation. Such are the crises of our times . . .

What is desperately needed is an *alternative reasoning process.* There have been some tentative steps in this direction: De Bono's "lateral thinking" and more recently "water logic"; Paul Tillich's "encompassing reason"; Habermas's "non-authoritarian dialectics"; Charles Handy's *Age of Unreason*; Bateson's "ecology of mind"; Lawrence Kohlberg's "higher moral integration"; and my own steps towards dilemma or issue resolution. The great psychologist William James was close to realizing the need for an alternative process when he wrote:

> He knows that he must vote for the richer universe, for the good which seems most organizable, most fit to enter into complex combinations, most apt to be a member of a more inclusive whole. [1943, p. 83]

But in my own view it was the poet and anthropologist Ruth Benedict who came closest to the elusive quest, only five days before her death. She had studied five American Indian tribes: three, suicidal, disintegrating, emiserated; two, healthy, high-spirited, and well-functioning. Over fifty "independent variables" thought to "cause" these differences had failed entirely to predict the outcomes. Benedict moved to a different paradigm. What mattered, she decided, was not the presence of a particular variable, say self-interest or altruism, but the *synergy between the two.* Societies were happy when the two values had been reconciled, miserable when each fought the other. Her unpublished papers were found by Abraham

Maslow, who made synergy the cornerstone of his theories. The individual must be reconciled to social concerns, he taught, altruism and egoism must co-evolve. Which brings us back to our welfare system and the need for a logic that transcends the warring "rationalities".

January 1994

FOREWORD

Ian Sparks

Director, The Children's Society

Any manager in the human services field could be forgiven for treating a book like this as if it were a hand-grenade with the pin pulled out! The human services field, whether in personal social services, health, education, or the voluntary sector, is bursting with pressures for change—budget reductions, compulsory tendering, trust status, performance audits, new legislation. We have so much to do, the last thing we need is an invitation to start thinking about what we do!

And yet... the world is not going to get any simpler or less demanding in the foreseeable future. If we do not manage our immediate world, it will end up managing us.

What I like about McCaughan and Palmer's book is that it relates to the world I live in as a manager, and it talks about ways of dealing with life that are located in a world I recognize.

They identify the tendency of senior managers to have "flavours of the month"—because they are interested in and stimulated by ideas—without understanding the effect these have on those further down the organization. The authors' cameos capture a world we all recognize, such as the meetings where "half of the team arrive late and breathless and the other half have negotiated to leave early".

For me in particular they take seriously the complexity of the world of management. I have worked in The Children's Society since 1981, and I have been its Director since 1986. Over that time I have learnt that managing an organization over seven years is very different from managing it for three years.

In the first three years there is an impetus for change which can produce the illusion that the organization is really moving forward. Over seven years you realize that deep-rooted change takes time and patience. One reason for this is that over the longer period you see and have to work with the longer-term (and perhaps unintended) effects of your earlier decisions. You also realize that working strategically involves thinking about everything at the same time, which is very hard work. I was pleased to see that one of the authors' principles is to enable managers to understand, enjoy, and deal with complexity.

The longer-term view also makes you realize that you have to work with the people you have. This may sound negative, but it is an important corrective to the view in the more excitable management books, that successful managers are the ones who sack the old team and bring in a new and more dynamic one. Not only is this unacceptable in the human services world; it also disregards the fact that we all have limitations and we all have potential.

We glibly say that staff are our greatest asset, but rarely make that specific and realize that the actual people we have around us are an asset, and need to be treated as such. Throughout this book the authors show how managers have been able to reframe their thinking, so that they work with the potential of people rather than longing for a more perfect world.

Perhaps the best thing about this book is that it shows how managers can work together, to help one another to work out their problems and develop their skills. In a world where a myriad of books offer us instant solutions from the "guru of the month", it is refreshing to read about and experience managers working together on real problems and helping each other move forward.

If it does nothing else, this book will help you to realize that within a chaotic and ever-changing human services world, it is possible to be in control and to manage your world, rather than allowing it to manage you.

SYSTEMS THINKING
FOR
HARASSED MANAGERS

INTRODUCTION

OUR PURPOSE

I n this book we set out to do three things:

1. to outline the elements of systems thinking in its application to organizations;

2. to describe a procedure, based on systems thinking, for addressing situations in organizations which are causing you problems.

3. to provide examples of managers using this procedure to tackle real situations, and so give you a glimpse of how you could work in this way yourself.

The examples are drawn primarily from our own work with managers in statutory and voluntary health and welfare organizations in Britain, many of them from our workshops on systems thinking. These concepts of systems thinking are, however, also being applied in business, education and government, the armed forces, churches and synagogues, and other types of organization, in many parts of the world.

The know-how we are talking about cannot be gained without practice, whether in work situations or in training workshops. This book contains "say-how" rather than know-how: it is an attempt to put into words, necessarily incompletely, concepts and principles that illuminate what managers and consultants do when they are using a systems approach. We envisage that some readers will use this book to develop and understand better what they are already doing; others will be stimulated by it to gain the know-how, at work and perhaps at some stage through formal training.

We are not attempting to give a comprehensive account of management or consultancy. This is simply a framework for defining, analysing, intervening in, and learning from problematical situations, one that might be adopted in a variety of consulting relationships:

- a manager or anyone else advising a subordinate, colleague, or other member of their immediate work unit: or a group, team, or committee;

- a manager or anyone else asked or offering to consult informally to a person or group outside their immediate work unit;

- a designated consultant, working within an organization for a salary, or called in from outside, for a fee or for free;

- a group of colleagues meeting together to support and advise each other, perhaps as an expression of a commitment to be or become a learning organization;

- a manager trying to sort out a problematical situation by in effect acting as a consultant to himself or herself—either alone, or using a friendly person as a sounding board.

The book is organized around the stages of the consultation process that we follow in our workshops and more freely in the course of our everyday work. We describe these workshops in more detail in the Appendix. The core activity is a group consultation, in which one participant on the workshop acts as presenter and puts forward a current work problem for analysis and interpretation by the other workshop participants, who act as consultants. The stages of the process are these:

1. *Clarifying*: understanding the nature of the problem as it is seen and presented by the manager.

2. *Questioning*: probing and developing the manager's description of the problematical situation.

3. *Hypothesizing*: generating models of the patterns of interaction which explain how the problem behaviour is perpetuated.

4. *Proposing interventions*: devising possible courses of action to resolve or dissolve the problematical situation.

We describe these stages in detail in chapters two to five. In chapter one we introduce some of the basic concepts of systems thinking in its application to organizations. In chapter six we expand on some key concepts introduced in the preceding chapters.

WHERE WE ARE COMING FROM

Our particular slant on systems thinking and its application in organizations reflects the routes by which we have come to be collaborating on this book.

Nano McCaughan became interested in systemic thinking and practice when she was a Development Officer with a local authority. She had occasion to talk to a child psychiatrist at a local child guidance clinic, who remarked that recent innovations in family systems thinking had connections with group theory, with which they were both familiar, but introduced new and fascinating differences. As a result of this conversation, the psychiatrist offered her the opportunity to take part in a weekly half-day session at the clinic.

She took up the offer eagerly and continued at the clinic for several years. During that time she attended a one-year part-time course at the Institute of Family Therapy, joining a group run by David Campbell employing the Milan approach to family therapy developed by Selvini-Palazzoli, Boscolo, Cecchin, Prata, and their collaborators.

Until 1981, when he launched out as a self-employed consultant, Barry Palmer had been working for the Grubb Institute, as a consultant to organizations and as a member of the group of colleagues who collectively managed its affairs. He had acted as a staff member and sometimes as director of a long series of workshops on group relations (called "working conferences"), which were based on the open systems model of organizations (see chapter one). Nano

McCaughan had also come into contact with the group relations workshops through her early groupwork training, and had taken part in them as a member and a staff member.

Barry Palmer's first encounter with the Milan approach was through a colleague, Bruce Reed, who had worked with Boscolo, Cecchin, and Borwick on using systemic concepts in the design of a management development programme for an international company (Wynne, McDaniel, & Weber, 1986, pp. 423ff) . Through Reed he became interested in the concepts of positive connotation and reframing (see chapter four). In group relations practice, restrictive and repetitive patterns of behaviour, in groups or organizations, were usually interpreted as manifestations of unconscious defence mechanisms. The Milan approach offered an alternative perspective.

"CHANGE WITHOUT CHAOS?"

In the early 1980s we began to collaborate in running workshops for managers, initially based on the group relations model. Then, in 1985, we decided to introduce participants to systems thinking as it had been developed in family therapy, and to work with them in using it to untangle their organizational problems. At the time of writing, we have run nine of these *Change Without Chaos?* workshops. We kept notes on the workshops, with varying degrees of thoroughness, and in due course realized that our increasingly bulging files might give birth to a book.

In writing this book, and in leading the workshops themselves, we have drawn upon the ideas and experience of many other writers and practitioners, including David Campbell, who acted as an adviser to us in the early stages; Bruce Reed and our other former colleagues at the Grubb Institute; Peter Lang and Martin Little at the Kensington Consultation Centre; Humberto Maturana and Karl Tomm, whose seminars we attended; Philip Boxer, with whom Barry has had a long and valuable association; and all the veterans of our workshops and members of the Systems Group to which they gave rise; and, through their writings, Gregory Bateson, Mara Selvini-Palazzoli and her collaborators, Paul Watzlawick and his collaborators, Fritjof Capra, Gareth Morgan, William Torbert, Peter Senge and Charles Hampden-Turner. Some of these influences will be apparent in what follows; those that are not, we gratefully acknowledge here.

We like the systems approach because it is an adult-to-adult approach. As we have used this method in our workshops, we have been able to work with the participants in a way that focuses upon their experience of their organizations, and upon the theory, rather than upon us as repositories of superior knowledge. It enables managers to engage with large problems without being overwhelmed by them, by discovering that problems can begin to shift when given a gentle nudge in the right place. It resists Utopianism and acknowledges the limits of our power. And it respects and seeks to understand what Bateson called the circuitry of organizations (i.e. their systemic structure), and of the society of which they are a part, before seeking to change them, rather than identifying causes and trying to eliminate them by force. In this sense, the sense in which Bateson also used this word, it is a wise approach:

> That is the sort of world we live in—a world of circuit structures—and love can survive only if wisdom (i.e. a sense or recognition of circuitry) has an effective voice. [1972, p. 146]

THE CASE MATERIAL

Much of the case material in this book is derived from consultations in our workshops. We have discussed our accounts of the more detailed cases with the people concerned; they have corrected inaccuracies and authorized us to use the material with suitable modifications to disguise its origins. (To our surprise, some of these telephone conversations have turned out to be significant interventions in themselves, triggering further action as well as satisfying our curiosity.) The names we have used are fictitious. This case material inevitably reflects the workshop context in which it was generated; but we wish to make it clear that we are not assuming that you, the reader, will be working in a group when you use the procedures and concepts outlined here. We hope that you are lucky enough to find the kind of stimulus and support that can arise in a group situation, but we appreciate that you may have to go it alone.

CHAPTER ONE

Going round in circles

Technical or formal rationality is linear: you reason, you act, you achieve accordingly. Encompassing reason is circular and iterative. You probe, discover something interesting, reflect, cogitate and probe again. The manager acts with whatever degree of forethought is appropriate, but carefully examines the feedback and, through a cybernetic process, rethinks and acts again, learning along the way.

C. Hampden-Turner, 1990, p. 5

Over the past nine years we have run a series of workshops in which managers have consulted each other about problem situations in their organizations. We have also acted as consultants to managers in a range of organizations, and have consulted each other and other people about our own work. This has given us a picture of the kind of circumstances in which managers and others become sufficiently perplexed or exasperated to seek an outsider's perspective on what is going on around them.

6

The problems themselves have been varied and complex. Many have reflected larger-scale pressures on the life and governance of organizations in Britain: pressures towards greater efficiency and value for money, flatter organizations, equality for disadvantaged groups, clearer accountability on the part of those who spend public and charitable money, and a sharper focus on the quality of provision for customers, clients, and service-users.

We have worked with directors, senior managers, and governing bodies directly concerned with formulating policies in these areas, but much of our time has been spent with the managers who have had to implement such policies. Many of these have identified themselves strongly with the harassed managers in the title of our workshops and of this book.

Some have been concerned with how to generate a sense of ownership of policies that are felt to have been imposed from above; how to implement policies for which—as they see it—there is limited support or even active opposition; how to enable people to keep their wits through what seems like continuous organizational and social change; and, *in extremis*, how to deal with angry and cynical staff.

Others have raised difficulties that were on the face of it more local: how to make a functioning team out of a collection of people who had stronger professional or ethnic allegiances elsewhere, or who did not see themselves as a team or were at daggers drawn; how to secure the co-operation of wayward or difficult team members; how to get voluntary workers or committee members to conform to the standards of practice desired by their salaried senior managers and perhaps by funding bodies; how to wind a unit down, or to set up a new one from scratch or by merging previously existing units with distinct histories and cultures; how to preserve continuity while key figures leave and new brooms sweep in.

What do these disparate problems have in common? We have become aware of these recurring themes:

- *Stuckness*: managers are faced with a state of affairs that they cannot accept, but which they are unable to shift. Whatever solutions they have tried have not worked, or are not working fast enough. Their bosses cannot help, or cannot be approached, or are part of the problem. They are going round in circles.

- *Politics*: many problems, as they are defined, hinge upon the manager's power, or lack of it, to influence other people to do what he or she believes is necessary. Sometimes the manager has formal authority but is uncertain how to exercise it; sometimes he or she is entirely dependent on the willing co-operation of others.

- *Complexity*: the situations described are invariably complex, both to grasp and to analyse. To understand what lies behind even a simple question like "How can I enable the staff to talk to one another and trust one another?" entails exploring a complex and ambiguous domain. It is necessary to take in a lot of information. It is also necessary to grasp what has been called the dynamic complexity (Senge, 1990, p. 71) of the underlying situation (this is discussed further in chapter two).

We have found that we, and the managers we work with, are able to gain leverage on the problems they present—to engage with them in a way that addresses the manager's stuckness, the politics, and the situation's dynamic complexity—if we examine what is going on from the perspective of systems thinking. This book is a demonstration of what we mean by adopting a systems perspective, and later in this chapter we explain what we mean by this. But first, here are accounts of two incidents, from our own experience, which may begin to give you a feel of systems thinking in practice.

A "DIFFICULT" INDIVIDUAL

Clive, the manager of a small research and development team in an impoverished social services department, was exasperated by a competent but uncooperative and evasive member of his team. She ignored the team's priority work in favour of projects of her own and was frequently out of the office and uncontactable. Nothing he had said in her supervision sessions had made any difference. The rest of the team were becoming resentful and demoralized.

Clive regarded his unit as a spearhead for change within the department. New legislation meant that big operational changes were in the offing, to which the director was strongly committed (though other managers were less enthusiastic). Clive's deadlines would have been tight even if all his team had been pulling their weight.

He consulted a group of participants on one of our workshops. They suggested that this was a normal state of affairs. They asked him more about the ambivalence about change in the department. It appeared that, while he was committed to change, others were putting the brake on. The group suggested that one way of reading this was that they were preventing the department from moving too fast. His uncooperative team member might be representative of a sizeable body of people who wanted to hold on to what was tried and familiar in their way of working.

The group went on to suggest a number of options for action, some of them mutually exclusive. One member suggested finding the difficult team member another job, another that Clive should start disciplinary proceedings. Another proposed that he should stop putting pressure on her and start to behave in a way that acknowledged her contribution to the work of the department as a valid and useful one.

The latter is what he in fact did. He redefined her job within the team, so that she could continue the kind of work she was familiar with and good at, and arranged for her to consult another assistant director about the deadlines she should work to—someone who would take the heat off her, because he was less anxious about the forthcoming changes than he was himself. In a short time she became a much more positive member of the team and even began to give some time to the research and development priorities.

* * *

What is going on here? It is significant to us that in discussion Clive begins to adopt a wider perspective on what initially seemed to be trouble with an uncooperative individual. To move or discipline (or sack) a "difficult" individual, as some people suggested, often seems the only solution and conforms to the popular image of the tough manager. But this would have left unaddressed the larger process of which this behaviour was a part: the department was torn between adapting to new circumstances and holding on to a sense of continuity and to what was good in the old way of doing things. Of course it might be suggested here that the manager caved in and accepted that he had one less person on the priority work. So his change of behaviour towards the team member may not have been wise, unless he had also had some tough conversations with his director about a pace of change that the department could sustain. This is an important element in systems thinking: that a change in one relationship within a system changes all the other relations too.

WHEN IS A TEAM NOT A TEAM?

Here is another example. A psychotherapist contacted one of us (BP) on behalf of a multi-disciplinary child guidance team based in a hospital. The team comprised psychotherapists, consultant psychiatrists, a social worker, an occupational therapist, a psychologist, and two administrators. They were having difficulty working together as a team and had obtained funding for an "awayday" in which to try to sort out their differences with a consultant.

The consultant had difficulty agreeing with them about achievable goals for the day, not least because every time he wrote or telephoned he found himself dealing with a different person. He asked every team member to write him a letter explaining what they saw their difficulties to be. When he had read them he wondered what on earth they could do about it all in a few hours.

On the day, he asked them for examples of what they regarded as teams. They said a football team, or the team in an operating theatre. He pointed out all the ways in which they were not like these teams: there was no goal that they were all shooting at; they worked with their clients only singly or in pairs, never all together; they were in different professions with different values and conventions; they had different bosses, different pay and conditions; one member, the social worker, was in a different organization from the rest of them. He asked why they didn't forget about being a team and regard themselves simply as colleagues who met periodically to discuss and co-ordinate their work with children.

Through the day the mood shifted. They had seen themselves as failures, unable to live up to their ideal of teamliness. Now they began to see themselves as achieving a modest but useful level of collaboration in the face of massive obstacles. What is more, they were working together very effectively at that moment, listening to each other, making inventive suggestions, ignoring differences of status. Before they went home, they had made various undertakings to each other about how they would modify their behaviour to strengthen their cohesion as a working group. In a letter to the consultant a year later, one of the psychotherapists said:

> We have started to put into practice some of the suggestions made, and have a special meeting now to raise difficult issues each week. I managed to arrange to see one less client so that I also have more time for meeting colleagues! Management are undoubtedly nervous about our newly strengthened cohesiveness, but it is clearly up to us to help them understand.

* * *

So there is a group of co-workers who create a new space for themselves—the "awayday", away from the hospital—in which a different pattern of working together can emerge. There is someone who sets out to help and gets entangled in their problems himself. There is an unexpected move, by which he gives them reasons for despairing of working together, rather than trying to give them hope. And there is a modest change, which leaves many problems unaddressed and disturbs another part of the system, but which is enough to set them on a new course.

SYSTEMS THINKING

What, then, is meant by the word "system"? A system is a set of components that make up a complex whole—a whole that is more than the sum of its parts. This is a general definition, for all kinds of system. The human body may be looked upon as a system, one whose components are its constituent cells. The body is more than an aggregate of cells: its qualities and capabilities could not be deduced from the properties of cells. Similarly the relations between the flora and fauna of a region can be better understood if they are seen as components of an eco-system. (In all these statements we have used phrases like "may be looked upon", "may be understood", because systems, like beauty, exist in the eye of the beholder. No system exists without someone who perceives or distinguishes the components as components of a larger whole.)

In the world of human associations like Marks and Spencer, the Beatles, The Children's Society, the Berlin Philharmonic, Dorset County Council, and our own teams and families, organization theorists have distinguished systems with various kinds of components: individuals and work units of various sizes, and also recurring behaviours or activities, sometimes conceptualized as roles. It is with this last type of system—systems as patterns of interaction—that we are primarily concerned. This strand of systemic thinking originated in the work of Gregory Bateson (1972) and has been influenced by the Milan school of family therapy (e.g. Selvini-Palazzoli, Boscolo, Cecchin, & Prata, 1980). From this point of view, a system is a pattern of interaction, between persons or groups, which can be represented by one or more *feedback loops*—that is, by closed loops or sequences of interaction that link and integrate all the components of the system. We say more about this concept in the next section.

So systems thinking is a way of describing and explaining the patterns of behaviour that we encounter in the life of organizations: the regularities of individual behaviour, which we describe as a role, the characteristic ways of doing things in organizations which we refer to as their culture, the repeating patterns of sterile conflict or mistakes or absenteeism or failure to delegate, which we define as problems and try to solve.

Once we have constructed models of the feedback processes that generate the behaviour we regard as problematic, we can use them to explain why our attempted solutions have failed to shift the problem, or have even perpetuated it, and to suggest other strategies that might have more leverage. Whether or not implementation of these strategies has the results we hoped for, it gives us more information about the system, so that we are able to construct new or modified models that explain more of what is going on. It is this process of observation, model-building (hypothesizing), and intervention that we shall be describing in this book.

LINEAR AND CIRCULAR PROCESSES

In order to understand the concept of systems as closed feedback loops, it is necessary to distinguish between linear and circular (or recursive) interactive processes. A few examples will demonstrate the difference. A woman is sitting with a cat on her lap; she is stroking the cat, and the cat is purring. The woman thinks: "The cat is purring because I am stroking him." This is a linear description: an effect (purring) is explained by means of a cause (stroking). The description is of the general form shown in Diagram 1.

strokes ————▶ purrs

Diagram 1

The cat has another view about it. He thinks: "The woman is stroking me because I am purring"—another linear explanation, but with a different view of cause and effect (Diagram 2).

strokes ◀———— purrs

Diagram 2

But it is possible for us to take a third view, from outside the system, and propose that each behaviour triggers the other, in a continuous process of circular causation (Diagram 3).

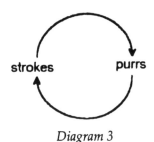

Diagram 3

One of the foremost authorities on circular causation is Hawkeye, one of the maverick doctors in the M*A*S*H television series. On one occasion Hawkeye and the Colonel are ambushed by the Chinese. The Colonel starts shooting back, but Hawkeye holds fire. When the Colonel asks him why he is not returning their fire, Hawkeye replies:

> The reason they shoot is because they're angry. If I shoot at them they'll get even more angry and shoot at us.

On another occasion Hawkeye and the Colonel have been helping out at an overworked South Korean field hospital. As they are
leaving, the hospital chief speaks to them:

Chief: Thank you for all your help.

Hawkeye: Thank you for all your wounded.

In our first case study, the uncooperativeness of the subordinate
was a response to the pressure of the manager, who was responding to her uncooperativeness, who was responding to his pressure
. . . Leaders of meetings complain that they can never start meetings
on time because people always come late . . . (work it out for yourself!).

One of the basic skills of systems practice (i.e. managerial or consultancy practice based on systems thinking) is the skill of recognizing these recursive processes, which go round in circles. The root
meaning of the word "recursive" is "running back". Systemic explanations "run back", in the sense that they double back on themselves, indefinitely, like one's reflection in two parallel mirrors. The
cat purrs because the woman strokes it, and the woman strokes
because the cat purrs, which is purring because the woman is stroking, and so on ad infinitum.

We have referred to these loops as *feedback* loops. Systems are
said to be structured by feedback. Norbert Wiener, the founder of
cybernetics, defined feedback in this way: "Feedback is a method of
controlling a system by reinserting into it the results of its past
performance" (1954/67, p. 84, cited in Keeney, 1983, p. 66).

Writers from Bateson (1979, pp. 196ff) onwards have used the
example of a thermostatically controlled heating system to demonstrate feedback. When the temperature falls below the limit at
which the thermostat is set, the boiler is triggered to turn on; in
other words, the result of its past inactivity—a cold room—is fed
back into the system and activates the boiler. When the temperature
of the room exceeds the set limit, the boiler is switched off.

Similarly, when one of us (BP), who is self-employed, is short of
work, he gives a lot of attention to pursuing new opportunities. As
new work—usually—comes in, he has less and less time for following up potential opportunities, to the point where he is flat out
dealing with existing commitments. This means that he gives little
attention to what he will be doing in six months' time, and when that

time arrives he is short of work. The results of his past performance are reinserted into the system of his work in an insistent way!

So a system is constituted and regulated by feedback. In fact, the system *is* this recursive pattern, just as a dance is the pattern made by the dancers. This has been expressed more elegantly by Gianfranco Cecchin (1987, p. 408): ". . . the system is simply doing what it does, and this doing is the it that does it."

ORGANIZATIONS

The systems concept provides our basic model of organizations and their constituent units. We start from the premise that organizations are real, and yet not real. They are real in the sense that they impinge, sometimes powerfully, on our lives; but they are not real, in the sense that they are not objects in the way the buildings they sometimes occupy are objects. "The world we know is not illusion, not real" (Keeney, 1983, p. 64). Language confuses us here, because we often use the same word to refer to an organization and to the building that houses it. If someone says, "I work for a bank", he does not mean he works for a building in the High Street, although if someone stopped him in the High Street and asked where the bank was, he would point to the building across the street.

Organizations exist for us because they are agreed to exist. When we talk about them we do so metaphorically: we refer to them by means of conventional images and models, which we assume the other person will recognize. (For a full account of this, see Gareth Morgan, 1986.) For example, if a manager says, "There are ten people in my department", we understand without thinking about it the way he or she conceives of the department as some kind of container that people can be "in". We are so used to this convention that we take it as a literal statement.

You may be wondering why we are making such a meal of this. The reason relates back to what we said earlier about the way problems are framed. For most of the time we take our department, say, as given. We plan and act on the assumption that it is an object independent of ourselves. But when we encounter problems "in" our department, our difficulty in finding an effective response may stem from the assumptions we have made about its reality—for example, about the boundary of this container and who is "in" it. If "in" means "on the current establishment and reporting to us", we may be excluding our predecessor, who is still very much "in" the department as far as our staff are concerned; or our clients, whose demands loom large in our staff meetings. One of us was advising the committee of a voluntary organization. Many of them expressed great relief that a committee member who had dominated their proceedings with his concerns had now resigned. We noticed that they spent a large part of the meeting deploring his behaviour and refuting his ideas.

Systems thinking provides ways of representing organizations, that is, of constructing metaphorical models of them in a more deliberate way. But while they may be more sophisticated than the metaphors of ordinary conversation, they are still metaphors, and as such they highlight some aspects of organizational life and overlook others.

ORGANIZATIONS AS SYSTEMS

The open systems model

There are at least two approaches to understanding organizations which are broadly systemic. One is the "open system" model, derived from the study of physical and biological systems and developed by, amongst others, Trist, Rice, Miller, and their collaborators at the Tavistock Institute of Human Relations (e.g. Miller & Rice, 1967). This model focuses upon the dynamic relationship between the organization and its environment, and it assumes that its continuing viability depends upon maintaining certain critical interchanges with that environment. The open system metaphor has now been widely absorbed into managerial thinking. It provides a powerful tool for representing the structure of an organization or part of it, for exploring the processes through which it achieves its aims and secures its viability, and for designing and testing alternative structures for performing different tasks. These critical aspects of managing and consulting are worth a book on their own, and indeed several have been written, including the one we have mentioned (Miller & Rice, 1967; see also Morgan, 1986, chapter 3).

The recursive systems model

The other approach, on which this book is based, represents organizations as patterns of feedback loops of the kind we have just described. This might be called the recursive systems model (cf. Reed & Armstrong, 1988, and Palmer & Reed, in preparation, in which the expression "containing systems thinking" is used). These feedback loops may incorporate pairs and sub-groups of those regarded as "in" the organization, or everyone "in" the organization, and/or others usually regarded as outside it—clients and customers, suppliers, competitors, government bodies, the media, or indeed any person or agency that can be seen to influence, or be influenced by, the organization's activities. As we shall see, formulating hypotheses to explain repetitive patterns in organizational life entails making decisions about "where to draw the line"—that is, whose influence to include in, and exclude from, the explanation of what is going on.

These feedback processes include those by which the organization as a whole retains its identity, in the eyes of those who have dealings with it. They manifest themselves in the culture of the organization—the characteristic ways of doing things, which distinguish one organization from another. One body of theory originating from Maturana and Varela (e.g. 1987) proposes that social systems like organizations are comparable to biological living systems like plants and animals, in that they have the capacity continuously to regenerate the relations by which they are constituted. They call this process "autopoiesis", which means "self-making". Thus the relations between the parts of a human individual, which make them recognizably the same individual throughout their life, are continuously maintained, even though there is a constant turnover of the body's constituent molecules; none of us is made of any of the same stuff after seven years. Similarly an organization is recognizable as the same organization, even after a 100% turnover of staff—provided they do not all leave at once!

Autopoiesis is the result of feedback processes, in the sense described above. The character of the organization remains constant, within certain limits, because deviations from the operative aims, rules, and culture of the organization are fed back into the system, triggering actions that correct the deviation. Employees who are repeatedly late get the sack; customers who do not pay their bills are taken to court.

Organizational learning

However, organizations and the people who work for them differ from humbler biological organisms in that they can learn. A tree can only become a bigger tree, but an organization can go through radical mutations, so that the aims, rules, and culture that control its autopoiesis themselves change over the years. Not all these can be attributed to organizational learning: some are the result of violent intervention—that is, of changes imposed from outside, often reflecting the political agenda of the day. The contemporary challenge to organizations to modify their aims, rules, and cultures *for themselves* has led to the current interest in organizational learning (e.g. see Garratt, 1990; Senge, 1990; Pedler, Burgoyne, & Boydell, 1991; Bazalgette & French, 1993). As the rate of change of the environment of organizations has increased, and the direction of this change has become increasingly unpredictable, there has been a growing recognition that the survival and continuing effectiveness of organizations in all sectors of society depends upon their capacity to learn. A learning organization supports the learning of its members, and is also capable of corporate learning, in the sense that it modifies its structure and practices, and the philosophy on which they are based, to meet changing conditions.

However, as Morgan has pointed out (1986, pp. 90ff), there are many processes in organizations which militate against developing the self-questioning culture of the learning organization:

- "impression-management": the methods by which managers and staff set out to make the situation look *better* than it is, rather than *as* it is;

- inattention to the gap between rhetoric and practice, or between what Argyris and Schon (1978) have called "espoused theories" and "theories-in-use";

- group influence: the considerable social rewards that come to those who do not challenge current practices.

Clearly, the ability of an organization to transform itself is hugely dependent upon the capacities and commitments of its leaders. These necessary qualities have been penetratingly explored by William Torbert (1991; Torbert & Fisher, 1992). We say more about his work, and about organizational change, in chapter six.

CONFLICT AND COLLABORATION

The story of the life of a team, a department, or an organization is one of interaction between persons and groups in conflict and co-operation. Men and women with diverse personalities and histories come together with the intention of realizing only partially convergent aims and interests. Managers seek by various means to mobilize cooperative activity around corporate aims and values to achieve agreed outcomes. To the extent that they are successful, those they manage subordinate other wishes, which are incompatible with the aims of the unit, to the achievement of those aims.

While shared aims may be the ideal, there is an important strand of thinking (e.g. Hampden-Turner, 1990) that places more emphasis upon the conflicting beliefs and ideologies that shape organizational affairs. These do not necessarily, or perhaps ever, add up to an integrated, consistent system of aims and values. Instead, individuals and groups are committed to an array of only partly compatible assumptions. As a result, managers find themselves confronted with apparently insoluble dilemmas, and they may lurch between one false solution and another, or become immobilized between factions representing different commitments. So, for example, social work organizations have over the years oscillated between structures based on generic and on specialist social work teams, as though one form of organization or the other could overcome all the difficulties of delivering social work services. On a larger scale, Boris Yeltsin has committed himself both to maintaining law and order in Russia and also to creating a democratic system of government. But it is unlikely that these two commitments are compatible in Russia as it is today. We discuss later how analysing stuck situations in terms of the dilemmas of those involved provides a way of releasing constructive action.

It is of course notorious that people in organizations resist change, and that while agreed changes are generally less stressful than imposed ones, no significant change is accomplished without shock, anger, and mourning. You can't make an omelette without breaking eggs. From a systemic point of view, we may say that individuals and the organizations with which they are associated are not distinct. As John Donne said, "No man is an Iland, intire of it selfe". Organizations confer an identity on their members, and insofar as they become attached to these identities, they resist changing them. So managing change entails providing space in which people can renegotiate their relatedness to the organization and at the same time evolve a new sense of themselves. This is an ideal: we are well aware that much organizational change is violent and does not provide this space. Systemic thinking is a way of bringing into view the rich network of connectedness that is at risk in organizational change.

Systems thinking is not just about solving problems—it is a more comprehensive discipline than that. But the wish to solve problems provides a strong motive for grappling with what is for many people an unfamiliar way of looking at things. Once you are hooked we hope you will continue to be drawn by the elegance of these ideas and practices and explore the wider relevance of systems thinking.

CHAPTER TWO

What's the problem?

The Cat only grinned when it saw Alice. It looked
good natured, she thought: still it had *very* long
claws and a great many teeth, so she felt that it
ought to be treated with respect. "Cheshire Puss,"
she began . . . "Would you tell me, please, which
way I ought to go from here?" "That depends a good
deal on where you want to get to," said the Cat.

Lewis Carroll, *Alice's Adventures in Wonderland*

Problems worthy
of attack
prove their worth
by hitting back.

Piet Hein, 1969

I n the Introduction we suggested a number of circumstances in
which someone might adopt a systemic approach to problematic situations: a manager advising a subordinate, a colleague,
or someone else in their immediate work group; a manager consulting informally to someone outside their work unit; an internal or

21

external consultant advising an organization; a group of colleagues meeting to support and advise one another; or an individual taking time out to think through a current difficulty and in effect act as a consultant to himself or herself.

In each of these situations the people concerned set out to address and if possible resolve a problem. Whether they are successful may depend not only upon the specific circumstances, and upon their specialist knowledge and skill, but also upon their attitude to problems in general. Problems can appear massive and immovable, but they can also melt away like the Cheshire Cat. Like organizations, they are not illusory, and yet not real. If a team is told that their unit will be closed unless they can raise new income to cover all their costs, and they behave as though this were all a dream, they are likely to be in deep trouble which is not a dream either. Yet this is a state of affairs that is only problematical because they see or feel it as a problem: a problem is always a problem *for someone*. Another team competing for the same funds might be glad to see the other team go. We shall propose that if we accept the problems we encounter as real—as ordinary cats rather than Cheshire Cats—we may be locking ourselves into impossibilities and throwing away the key.

SNARES

Nevertheless, organizational problems, like the Cheshire Cat, are not as easily disposed of as the Red Queen thought. The Cat's head appeared in the air over the looking glass game of croquet:

> The Queen had only one way of settling all difficulties, great or small. "Off with his head!" she said, without even looking round.

In the early stages of a consultation, whether in the workshops or in any consultancy assignment, there are several snares, all of which can be seen as consequences of a Red Queen approach:

- We look no further than the presenting problem, and so propose quick-fix, symptomatic solutions that leave unaddressed the larger dysfunctional processes that are giving rise to the problem we are worried about. We allow staff to work longer and longer hours to meet increasing demands for services, rather than grasping the nettle of reassessing priorities. We pump up the tyre rather than fix the puncture and are puzzled when it is flat again the next morning.

- We attribute all the difficulties to a blameworthy individual (or group), whose behaviour has to be changed. So we sack difficult people, or send them on training courses, without investigating how the circumstances of their jobs may be provoking them to protest. This is a variant of our first snare, in which the presenting problem is a difficult individual or group.

These solutions often compound the problem they are intended to solve. In our first example in chapter one, Clive's criticism of a disaffected team member made that member even more disaffected and determined not to conform. A newspaper article (Garlick, 1990) describes how a community was attempting to deal with prostitution through the courts, by fining prostitutes for soliciting. The effect of this on women living on or below the poverty line was predictable: they were, the article says, "back on the streets within the hour, working to pay off the penalty". It is easier for us to find someone to blame, and become preoccupied with them, than to examine how our own efforts are themselves compounding the difficulties we are trying to overcome. We shall talk later about the contribution of Peter Senge to systems thinking. "There is no blame", is one of his laws of systems thinking (1990, p. 67).

- We struggle to no avail against persistent problems, without noticing that we have defined the problem in such a way that it can never be resolved. In our second example in chapter one, a group of colleagues were castigating themselves for not working together as a team, without noticing that their idea of what it meant to work as a team could never be realized in their circumstances.

- As a result of defining a problem unwisely, we apply our thought and energy in the wrong place or at the wrong level. One of us [BP] was asked to advise a health authority manager about a community mental health centre in which there was persistent conflict between two team leaders. We concluded that the source of their conflict lay in unresolved differences between administrative and clinical staff at a more senior level in the organization. The team leaders were re-enacting these differences. As long as the manager continued to worry about her team leaders, the differences at higher levels in the hierarchy went unaddressed. (We have called this defining the problem "unwisely". But since she would probably not have relished confronting her own senior managers, there may have been an unconscious wisdom in the way she constructed her problem.)

HARD AND SOFT PROBLEMS

Peter Checkland has distinguished between what he calls hard problems and soft problems (1981, p. 316). A hard problem is one concerned with finding an efficient means of achieving an identified and desired end result. For example, how can we arrange our staff meetings in this residential home, so that staff working both day and night shifts will be able to attend? The value of staff meetings is not in question: the only problem is how to organize them.

A soft problem is one in which purposes, goals, and desired end results are themselves problematic. There is a problem about defining the problem. In the extreme case the manager has a sense of malaise, or, more positively, of what Charles Kingsley called "divine discontent", about the present state of affairs but cannot express this in terms of a problem at all. Checkland gives as an example of a soft problem this question: what should we be doing about our inner city schools? The question of what to do about inner city schools implies dissatisfaction with the schools as they are at present, but this would leave a consultant with a lot of work to do to establish what they were expected to achieve and how they were falling short.

MALFUNCTIONS

So problems are not as solid as they sometimes appear. Using the noun "problem" can itself delude us into thinking that a problem is an objective thing. But, as consultants, our capacity to enable a client to discover new options is limited if we are unable to turn nouns back into verbs and recognize that what we are up against is someone who is *problematizing* the situation in which he or she has to act.

This recognition is central to the work of family therapists Peter Bruggen and Charles O'Brian (1987, pp. 226f). They distinguish between a "malfunction" and a "complaint". A malfunction is a state of affairs that is agreed to be a hard problem: the washing machine has broken down, staff meetings are incapacitated by absentees. We know what it would be like for the washing machine to function properly or for the staff meetings to be properly attended. "Complaint" is a more dynamic concept. Interestingly, in ordinary usage the word "complaint" can refer both to an unwelcome condition (like catarrh or eczema), and also to a communication about a condition ("I wish to make a complaint"). In this second sense, a complaint is something that occurs in a conversation. My broken washing machine becomes a complaint when I telephone the engineer. For some complaints there is no corresponding clearly defined malfunction; and in the world of organizations, as opposed to that of manufactured gadgets, what counts as a malfunction is always a matter of judgement, because the purpose of a meeting or project or procedure may be seen differently by different people.

Bruggen and O'Brian say they feel uncomfortable when the client and the complainant are not the same person—for example, when they are asked to see a family by a third party. They are uncomfortable because this invites them to accept the family as a problem, without access to the one who has defined them as a problem. One of us [BP] was once asked for help by the chair of the management committee of a voluntary hostel for offenders. She said the committee were concerned about the warden of the hostel, who concealed what was happening in the hostel from the committee and, they believed, became too emotionally involved with some of the residents. Would we see him? Fortunately, we recognized that it was the committee who were the problem-owners, not the warden. For all we knew, the warden might be quite satisfied with his work. (As it turned out later, the warden did have a problem: it was the committee.)

One of us had a dog called Joe whom the family thought very stupid. When we pointed at a ball on the other side of the lawn and said, "Fetch!", he would look at the hand which was pointing and not at the ball. Now, we think he would have made a good consultant.

PROBLEMS ARE MADE AND NOT BORN

So problems do not come into existence independently of us: they are created in our minds and in our conversations. Washing machines that don't wash and salespeople who don't sell are innocent in themselves: they are only problems to those who expect something different of them. This analysis suggests that the way a problem is defined is shaped by two things:

- the *aims and wishes* that are motivating the problem-owner to act;
- the *context* in which the problem-owner defines the problem, and in particular the way he or she perceives the one to whom the complaint is addressed.

The first point is obvious. The arrangement of pieces on a board which is called a chess problem is only a problem for me when I accept the challenge to checkmate the black king in three moves. Otherwise it is just an arrangement of pieces. The second point is a reminder that it is wise to ask prospective clients why they have chosen us as consultants. The client's answer may throw light on the way their perception of our knowledge and ability is shaping the way they define the problem. To adapt the old adage, if we are famous for our hammer, people will bring us nail-shaped problems.

DYNAMIC COMPLEXITY

The reader may be impatient with this analysis, feeling that in most situations it is enough to tackle the problems that are real to the client, in the terms that they are presented. We accept this, in the sense that there are occasions when we too take the presented problem at its face value and try to help the complainant solve it. But managers tend to consult colleagues or outside consultants when common-sense solutions have failed. They have taken the problem at its face value, and their solutions have been ineffective or have even made things worse. Many problems have what Senge (1990, p. 71) calls "dynamic complexity", and it is these for which a systemic approach may have a better chance of bringing about change.

Senge suggests that problems require special attention when they reach a certain degree of complexity, and that there are two types of complexity: *detail complexity* and *dynamic complexity*. Working out the timetable for a large school, specifying which classes will be studying which subjects, with which teachers, in which classrooms, during each period of the week, is a task presenting detail complexity. Detail complexity can be addressed with suitable procedures. (In the case of school timetables, we are told that even computers cannot do it—only a deputy head will do!)

Dynamic complexity is something different. Senge would be talking about dynamic complexity in situations when the same action leads to dramatically different results in the short and long term; or when an action has one set of consequences locally and another further afield; or when, as we have been discussing here, obvious interventions produce non-obvious results. If I find that the more persistently I go into my teenage son's bedroom and wake him up for school, the longer he takes to get up, I know that I am dealing with a situation of dynamic complexity.

UNMAKING PROBLEMS

It follows from this analysis that there are two ways a problem can be considered resolved:

- when the circumstances change or are changed, in ways that remove the perceived malfunction;

- when the problem-owner ceases to see the circumstances as problematical, or ceases to look for a helper.

Our case-study involving Clive in chapter one is an example of the first kind of outcome. The "difficult" individual became a more positive team member and began to give some time to priorities other than her own.

Here is an example of the second type of outcome. One of us [BP] was consulted by Gillian, the team leader of a voluntary project. The project was threatened with closure by its national organization, which had concluded that it could no longer provide the funding the project required. The project was faced with becoming self-financing within a year, or being closed down. In the first part of the consultation, Gillian ran through all the revenue-raising initiatives she and her team had thought of, all of which seemed forlorn hopes. There seemed to be no way forward. As the consultation continued, however, she stopped fending off the idea of closure and came to accept it as the most likely outcome. In other words, although not welcoming it, she ceased to focus upon it as a problem she had to solve. She concluded that her priority should be to use her therapeutic understanding of the mourning process to enable the project's clients and staff to terminate their relationship with it in a constructive way. She would still pursue some fund-raising initiatives, in case she was being pessimistic, but without being attached to the outcome.

* * *

In our workshops for managers we have found Watzlawick's distinction between a difficulty and a problem illuminating (Watzlawick, Weakland, & Fisch, 1974). In his language, a difficulty is an undesirable state of affairs, which can either be resolved by common-sense action, or which has to be accommodated to and lived with, because it is part of life and there is no known solution. A problem is an impasse that is created, perpetuated, and often made worse by mishandling a difficulty.

Watzlawick gives the example of alcoholism. Alcoholism can be seen as a serious social problem. But if the attempt is made to eliminate it through prohibiting the sale of alcohol, the cure turns out to be worse than the disease, as was found in the United States in the 1920s. The ban makes people more aware of their desire for drink, entrepreneurial ingenuity is mobilized to satisfy it, and alcoholism increases. In the attempt to stop this, the forces of law and order clamp down even more strongly, but with the effect of compounding the problem rather than eliminating it. Low-grade alcohol becomes an additional public health problem, and there is widespread corruption, smuggling, and gangland warfare. This is what Watzlawick calls a "more-of-the-same" solution: we discuss its dynamics in chapter four.

The problem of drug abuse turns out to be similar. In a published interview, the dramatist David Hare asks Mary Tuck, a former Head of Research at the Home Office, whether she would decriminalize drugs. She replies:

> Oh, without doubt. It's precisely the same question as with Prohibition in the Twenties. Look at America. You create a gang

culture in which all exchange is at the point of a gun. The natural pricing mechanism of the market is destroyed. You have prostitution, burglary, house-breaking, all to finance the artificially high price of the commodity. You destroy South American countries, you create an intolerable burden of enforcement costs which no society can afford. In America, the inner cities are totally destroyed and handed over to criminals, all to protect the price of crack and heroin. [Hare, 1993, p. 91]

Does this mean that it is better to do nothing about alcoholism or drug abuse? Not necessarily; but to be better than doing nothing, any strategy must start by defining the problem in a way that accepts that certain levels of alcohol abuse and drug abuse are inevitable in the kind of society we live in—that they are "difficulties" of our society.

BEGINNING

So how do we respond when someone presents us with a more or less clearly defined problem and asks for our help in tackling it? In the next chapter we discuss how we can begin to uncover through skilful questioning what we are being asked to address. For now, we are simply concerned with the consultant's stance. If we are naive at the beginning we may find ourselves in a morass later. (Even if we are smart at the beginning we may find ourselves in a morass later, but if we understand what is going on when problems are defined we have a better chance of extricating ourselves.)

In a nutshell, the challenge is to attend to at least three things at once:

- to the picture of the client's situation which unfolds;
- to the way the client builds up this picture, in his or her initial statement and in the continuing conversation;
- to the way we ourselves respond and contribute to this process.

We cannot think about all these things simultaneously, but we can learn to keep an eye on each of them as the consultation continues. For example, let us imagine that a project leader in a voluntary organization states his problem to a consultant in this way, as he did in one of our workshops: "How can I enable the members of my staff to talk to one another and trust one another?" We notice first of all the beginnings of a picture being presented. It is one in which all is not well between the staff: they are not talking to each other and do not trust each other. Secondly, we register that this is the *client's* picture of what is going on: we do not know whether other members of the project would say this, or whether we would say this if we visited them. The client's story in some way reflects his concerns, his aims and wishes, which as yet we do not know much about. It may also reflect his view of us and what he thinks will secure our interest or support. He is talking about a malfunction, but what we are hearing is a complaint.

Thirdly, if we are alert to our own responses—to what we feel about the client and his story, and to what we say or ask about it— we may also register how we are perhaps getting drawn into the story, accepting that the staff are mistrustful and agreeing that this is a bad thing, or rejecting the client and his story and taking up a critical posture. It will be by being alert to this level of the drama that we are enabled to adopt a systemic approach to the client's situation.

THE TENSION BETWEEN
LISTENING AND INTERVENING

So at this stage we are seeking both to listen to the client's description of his or her situation, and also to position ourselves in relation to it. If we are too busy asking questions and proposing formulations of the problem, we may muffle the voice of the client's concern, which we should not equate with the problem that is initially posed to us. If on the other hand we simply listen and take the situation as it is presented, we may in effect buy in to a formulation of a problem that is itself the problem. This is one of the snares we listed at the beginning of this chapter. Or we may fail to clarify in what way the problem described is the responsibility of the client, with the risk of spending a lot of time elucidating a situation in which the client is powerless to intervene. This is not to say that simply listening is in itself a mistake: it is possible to listen without buying in to the client's judgement of what is problematical. But this entails maintaining the kind of distance that enables us to take in the picture being painted, while remembering that it is the client's picture, painted from a particular position in a particular style. Simply listening is not always easy.

In our workshops we notice that managers have difficulties with positioning themselves in relation to the situations presented by their fellow workshop members. They use information shrewdly and ask sharp questions, but they too readily accept the picture they are offered and tacitly endorse the presenter's judgment about what is wrong. This is wholly understandable: they are colleagues in the workshop, often in the same kind of work, and they readily identify with the trials of the presenter. It is satisfying for consultants and client as it were to sit side by side and analyse a malfunction that is safely "over there". Sometimes they come up with good ideas; but they also set limits to what they can achieve. For if the behaviour of the presenter is itself part of the pattern of interaction that perpetuates the dysfunction, they will be unable to see or say this.

This difficulty is not restricted to the special circumstances of workshops. Anyone acting as a consultant, formally or informally, makes conscious or unconscious decisions about how they position themselves in relation to the client and his or her story. For the inside consultant the difficulty may be to see as *constructed* a picture that corresponds at certain points to his or her own organizational reality: the client says the boss is incompetent, and this is what the consultant thinks too. For the outside consultant the difficulty may be to see as constructed a problem that he or she has undertaken— or is seen as having undertaken—to *solve*. But the idea of being "inside" or "outside" is itself a construction, which disappears in (recursive) systemic thinking. Systems practice entails accepting the client's description as information while continuing to work at formulating hypotheses, which include the behaviour of the client in the processes represented. This is the subject of a later chapter (chapter four).

CHAPTER THREE

Asking the right questions

> Where people wish to attach, they should always be
> ignorant. To come with a well informed mind, is to come
> with an inability of administering to the variety of
> others, which a sensible person would always wish to
> avoid. A woman especially, if she have the misfortune of
> knowing anything, should conceal it as well as she can.
>
> Jane Austen, *Northanger Abbey*

Wisdom in human affairs seems to be a matter of asking the right questions. A "well-informed mind" can be an obstacle to insight, and an ability to turn one's ignorance into questions can be a priceless skill. In consultancy, questions perform several functions. In investigating any situation presented by a client, our questions have two overarching purposes:

- to enable the consultant (and the manager seeking advice) to arrive at hypotheses about why the situation is the way it is;

- to lead the manager (and the consultant) to see the problem situation from new perspectives, and "reframe" the goings-on they regard as problematical. In this sense every question is also an intervention.

In this chapter we discuss the kind of questioning through which these purposes can be achieved. We illustrate this almost entirely from our workshop experience, since it is in this context that we have kept the most detailed notes. But the principles are applicable anywhere.

LISTENING AND CLARIFYING

First there is a story to tell. Managers describe situations that they feel should change but will not, or will change but should not. Their feelings can range from a sense of mild malaise to acute worry and concern. In moving into a consultation, we invite managers to tell the story in their own way, and we try to understand what is that person's perception of the events and the meaning that is created for them. Quite often we hear first about a belief that the situation has been caused by one particular person or action. We do not directly challenge the interpretation put on the events. We are trying to engage with the client system, as well as understand the nature of the undesired situation. This means trying to hold a delicate balance between looking and acting interested, curious, concerned, and supportive and attempting to probe for bias, omissions, and personal judgements.

On our workshops, some managers have framed the position very precisely—almost as if they know what should be done but would like some consultation about what steps to take.

* * *

Alethea, the team manager of a large staff group, summarized the situation she wished to work on in this way:

It has taken me three years to build a cohesive team of disparate groups of staff, following a re-structuring. Now I have to amalgamate with another small group of staff who are reluctant and totally demoralized. How can I do this effectively?

Michael, a senior officer in a Local Authority Social Services Department, asked:

What can I do, given the organizational objectives and constraints, to create some personal space?

Others' problems are not so specific and require more unpacking:

The Children's Division of Exchester Social Services has a constant atmosphere of conflict and tension which is talked about but never yet resolved. The feeling is that this holds us back from progressing. How can I positively influence the situation—am I the problem or is it the organization?

Another, from Thomas, which at first seemed strange to the consultants, was:

How does the organization both leave me free to do my own thing and simultaneously serve to block me?

* * *

In order to enable participants in our workshops to grasp the steps in the consulting process, we punctuate it into periods of asking questions, framing hypotheses, and suggesting possible lines of action to the manager who has opted to be the consultee. We often make a further, artificial division in the questioning, between an initial "clarifying" stage, in which a preliminary sketch is built up, and then the questioning stage proper, in which we explore the underlying processes and meanings through systemic questioning. This is, however, no more than a teaching device; in the workshops and in our everyday work every question may draw out more information about what is going on, or provoke the manager to see the situation differently, or both. We have our intentions, which shift as the interview continues, but we can never know what effect our questions will have, because we have no way of knowing the message or meaning they will convey, particularly to a stranger of whose belief systems and contexts we are unaware.

Who, what, where, when, and how many?

The first step is therefore to clarify the bare bones of the situation as the manager sees it. We may not have to ask many questions; or, if we do, they are "factual" questions about who, what, where, when, and how many, filling in gaps in the manager's story. We have put "factual" in inverted commas, because further questioning generally reminds us that "facts" are not as solid as they seem. At this stage we are doing no more than building up a preliminary sketch we can work with.

This initial questioning establishes the manager's view of how long the situation has been developing; what the key historical events are; who the relevant actors are and at what level in the organization; and what the presenter's responsibility is for the situation, as he or she sees it. We also ask the manager what steps he or she has taken to deal with the problem so far, and with what results. This is important, and it requires some discipline to remember to find out about this, rather than being preoccupied with incipient solutions that may be occurring to you. In the workshops, some managers do not particularly like having to ask for consultation. They may be tempted to withhold information and then, when presented with hopeful interventions at the end of a consultation, to say: "Well, we tried that and it didn't work."

In the early stages, the exploration is generally helped by:

1. Being practical and specific and exploring around the problem situation. We might ask things like: When did the situation start? What was happening around that time in the team? What was happening in the wider organization?

2. Asking for clear descriptions of what people say and do—perhaps for what a colleague, James Wilk, calls "video-descriptions". If they are said to be anxious, or afraid, or hostile, or incompetent, how do they manifest this anxiety, fear, hostility or incompetence? What would we see and hear on the tape? This is not as simple as it might seem, particularly when speaking to the person concerned. There are social norms governing the way we should respond to people who express feelings. If a manager says, "I am extremely depressed about my team", we may feel we should sympathize with him or her, or just pass over the statement. It may seem brutal to raise questions like: "What does this depression lead you to do, or stop you from doing?"

3. Probing any tendency to scapegoat individuals and locate team and organizational problems in one person. If one person is said

to be rubbishing everyone else's ideas, how often do they do this, and where, and in what circumstances? What else do they do that is destructive? What do they do that is constructive? Establishing that the problem behaviour is only manifested for about 1% of the working day rather than 99% is a good way to challenge an existing organizational myth.

SYSTEMIC QUESTIONING

We then ask those participants who have taken on the role of consultant to discuss, in pairs, two or three questions they think it would be vital to explore. This is a good discipline, as the limitation to the number of questions forces concentration on developing an incipient hypothesis. This could also be a useful discipline for a team trying to develop their systems thinking skills by working on their own situations or cases.

The aim of systemic questioning is to try to grasp the hidden order of the organization; to probe the relationship, if any, between overt and covert rules and policies; to see problems and puzzles as symptoms of something else; and to enable managers to understand, enjoy, and deal with complexity, rather than reduce it by mechanisms of projecting blame onto individuals. It is a way of checking for linkages between people and events. It is also an opportunity to explore what the manager's story may be leaving out: there are usually some important connections that are not made until the right question is asked, or details that the manager may feel embarrassed about and wish to evade. As we noted in chapter two, problems are constructed by people. Managers present situations that they feel are stuck; a fresh look at the situation by a group or individual can often help to reframe the managers' understanding, so that they feel differently about it, are less troubled by it, and can "move on".

Questioning approaches the formulation of systemic hypotheses from various directions. We have distinguished the following purposes:

- establishing circuitry;
- establishing patterns;
- exploring meaning;

- exploring covert rules;
- exploring the time dimension.

We discuss each of these strategies in the following sections.

ESTABLISHING CIRCUITRY

Some questions are designed with the intention of raising the awareness of feedback processes—what Bateson called "circuitry"—in the minds of the consultant and client. Mutual influence in the patterning of events can be discovered by asking such questions as: "When A does . . ., what do you do?" "What does A do next?" "What does B do then?"

* * *

Peter was a manager of a small team in a local authority. He asked for some advice about managing a staff group of four, one of whom, Mary, was not functioning adequately. He was questioned about the behaviour of Mary in comparison with the others whose work was acceptable. He was also questioned about what he did in response to each of the complaints he was raising. These were some of the questions asked:

- Could you describe Mary's day? (The team manager had little information about that.)
- What are your expectations of Mary?
- Does she know this, and if so how?
- How do you respond when she fails to complete an assignment?
- Have you considered taking disciplinary action?
- If Mary were here, what would she say about your behaviour as a manager towards her?

These questions caused the manager to realize by implication that he was not giving a clear enough direction and feedback to this team member. He was able to give good advice to himself about what he might do in future.

* * *

Sarah was concerned about a long-term member of staff, Robert, whom she had inherited three years ago when she took over the project. Robert, although a senior project worker, was not turning up to staff meetings, seemed resistant and unhappy with a new regime and direction, and was actively encouraging rebellion in the young people who were the project's clients.

The consultant's questions did not take for granted the assumptions Sarah was making in telling her story:

- For whom is Robert's behaviour creating problems—other staff, young people, outside contacts?

- What else would have to change in order for Robert to change?

- Can you tell us what Robert does well and how you reward him, as well as what he does that makes you angry?

- How would other staff describe your relations with Robert?

- What would the young people say positively and negatively about Robert if you were to ask their opinion?

- If, in spite of this consultation, there is no difference in Robert's behaviour, what do envisage will be the consequences in two years' time?

- If you were Robert, what would you say was causing you problems about the staff meetings? (It seemed that it might be the intellectual content—his strengths lay in practical tasks and in relating to young people.)

The general drift of these questions was shaped by Sarah's answer to the first one. Sarah had honestly to admit that no one else was worried about Robert's behaviour, and that he was close to the young users, understood their needs, and was generally well respected by them. As a result of this session Sarah appeared to cool down about Robert. Three months later she said casually that he was no longer much of a problem, other issues having become more important.

* * *

The consultants usually have some leading to do to elicit clear descriptions of problems of actual behaviours, rather than predicates like "he is devious" and "I am overwhelmed". Questions such as "What exactly did he do that you consider devious; what evidence have you?", or "What does your feeling of being overwhelmed prevent you from doing that you would like to do?", can elicit a more specific description. In this way, over time, managers come to see more clearly how they are always involved in co-constructing situations.

ESTABLISHING PATTERNS

Other questions begin to draw out the patterning of relationships around particular situations under discussion. In any large organization, practically everyone has a layer of colleagues who are above them in the hierarchy and a layer who are below them, as well as others at their own level. Problems often arise because somebody is losing out in another context in another layer. For example, it is common for senior managers to feel a pressure to blame subordinates unjustly for decisions that the managers themselves originally promoted, but for which they are now being criticized by a powerful colleague.

Questions showing how the three layers are connected begin to clarify the weave of interpersonal relationships around the situation. Sometimes they show up skewed power and authority relations in the organization, where some managers are passed over, excluded from the information and decision-making that should rest with their role position. The dimensions that seem to be useful to enquire around in this context are power and intimacy.

Power

To explore power relations, we ask questions such as these:

- Who has the most power in the team? Who has the least? What methods do they use?
- Who makes coalitions with whom? Who is against whom? Where does the decision-making power lie in relation to the problem—in the team or elsewhere?

* * *

Ella's situation provides an example of questioning that totally changed the manager's understanding of a problematic situation (see also Palmer & McCaughan, 1988). For completeness we shall describe the whole consultation.

Ella presented her difficulty initially as a conflict between herself and a colleague from a neighbouring probation team, who was co-working with her in a client group. In exploring this relationship, questioners also asked about other relations at different levels; for example: Who supervised the group? Did the supervisor feel closest to Ella or Mike (the co-worker)? How did their two team leaders work together? Was there a difference in power and influence between the two teams? Which was seen as the most successful and by whom? Ella's honest answers revealed more about the context of the dyadic work relationship.

There was overt and painful conflict between the three probation teams in this region. Ella's team had been set up with a special remit to develop community approaches to work with offenders in the neighbourhood. In two years they had had no visible success, and individual caseloads had had to increase in the other two teams. Some of the original team members committed to community work had become demoralized and left. Others had joined the team who doubted the feasibility of the concept, including Ella. The other two teams were scathing about the team's failure. Additionally, there were now splits within the team, principally between Ella and another officer, Laura, who was the originator of the project and its strongest adherent. Mike was close to Laura. One hypothesis was obvious: frustration about a failing project was finding expression in a conflict between teams, and the conflict between Ella and Mike concealed the more damaging differences between the two factions in Ella's team.

The consultants suggested to Ella that she might:

- ask for a special meeting with Mike to discuss their unsatisfactory working relationship;
- invite a third person to be present (to prevent them getting stuck in a repetitive argument);
- ask Laura to be the third person;
- after this meeting, arrange for Mike and Ella to discuss the outcome with Ella's supervisor, who was also her team leader.

This was intended to address the situation at several levels. It would set up a potentially more constructive meeting between Mike and Ella. It would bring Ella and Laura closer together in solving a professional problem (their co-working relationship). And it would give the team leader, who was new, a handle on the situation.

A month later, on the second part of the course, Ella reported that she had arranged the two suggested meetings. The effect of interrupting the existing pattern of relations had been to open up the whole question of the team's mixed feelings about the project. The team leader had asked for Ella's advice in arranging a special review meeting of the project's work. It was agreed by the team that the continuation of the special project was impractical in the face of continued pressure of individual referrals, the refusal of senior managers to release team members from other statutory duties, and the team members' general lack of skill and experience in community work. Further questioning revealed that the whole idea of community work had been a contentious one, introduced by an ambitious assistant chief probation officer at the behest of his chief, who was not really committed to the ideas. In the end, the problem was reviewed at chief officer level, and the idea of a special team in community work was dropped.

* * *

Questions about power bring illuminating answers. Seemingly weak or vulnerable people can actually be quite powerful at times (as the parents of many three-year-old children will know). This is because of the feelings of protection they can arouse in others, and the creation of what Eric Berne (1966) refers to as "protection rackets". We are referring not just to the legitimate, overt power that is supposed to reside in lines of authority, but to the personal resourcefulness and dominance of individuals, who may be given power by others to challenge the organizational structures.

One common problematic situation about authority can arise when a team leader is appointed from outside for a team where one or more long-serving members had applied for the job. Often they have not come to terms with their disappointment or resentment at not getting the appointment, even though on the surface their behaviour may seem welcoming and helpful. A combination of the vulnerability and uncertainty felt by the newcomer, and the over-critical watchfulness and testing out by erstwhile rivals, can lead over time to the team leader becoming increasingly incompetent, with devastating consequences.

Intimacy

It may also be useful to explore attachments in the team. Bob Garratt (1990) points out that senior managers cannot function unless they are accepted by their colleagues. Otherwise, they can be denied the crucial information they need to work effectively. Social psychologists have described the affective needs of human beings in organizations. Individuals struggle to find the best balance for themselves to satisfy basic group needs in their own unique way. Close friendships or erotic attachments have powerful effects on role behaviour and arouse feelings of jealousy, exclusion, and suspicion in those not part of the attachment. This can be true of couples at work, however much the pair may try to give their relationship a low profile.

Questions that draw this dimension out are: Who is closest to whom? Who is friendly outside work? What difference does that make? Who always supports whom? Who is suspected of having a secret relationship with whom? Are there any particular closenesses in the relationships which cross hierarchical levels?

EXPLORING MEANING

Other dimensions of questioning begin to unfold the organizational story, as well as the interpersonal one. These questions try to expose and clarify the belief systems that are overtly and covertly operating and cause the problem behaviour.

Cronen and Pearce (1980) have developed a framework for analysing communication which they call the theory of the Co-ordinated Management of Meaning (CMM). The theory proposes that, in their dealings with one another, people in a system "co-create" their reality, with all its complexities, puzzles, and problems. They ascribe meaning to what is happening between them, by reference to one or more contexts that they assume they share. By evoking these contexts through their interaction, they co-create the reality in which they meet. So, for example, if one person asks another to undress, this request will have a different meaning according to whether they co-create their context as one of tailor or dressmaker and client, doctor and patient, or lover and lover. The trouble starts when they understand the context differently.

Cronen and Pearce propose that these contexts of meaning are hierarchically organized, so that each level is the context for the interpretation of others. Any two levels in the hierarchy are connected; they mutually influence each other. The number and nature of the embedded levels is not fixed, as our illustrations will show. Our (freely adapted) diagram of the levels that might be evoked in dealings between people in an organization is presented in Diagram 4.

The first level of the hierarchy is that of *content*—the content of any communication. The second is that of the *speech act*. Speech acts are "the things one person does to another by saying something" (Cronen & Pearce, 1980, p. 132): for example, I persuade, implore, threaten, or promise something to you. Next you respond to my speech act, not necessarily to the content or meaning I intended, but

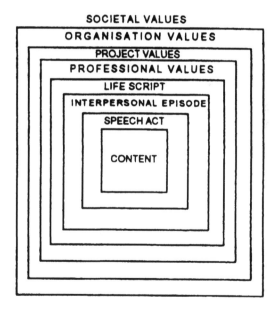

Diagram 4

to your reading of it. I in turn respond to you, and so progressively we enact a little scene that Cronen and Pearce call an *interpersonal episode*—a dress-fitting session, a medical examination, a seduction. In relations between people in organizations who interact frequently, these episodes often follow a similar pattern and, for example, can lead to familiar quarrels about budgets, permissions, or lateness. If this interaction is between a man and a woman, the meaning of it to the participants might be shaped by beliefs higher up the hierarchy of contexts—perhaps in the *family life scripts* of the participants ("mother never stands up to father") or in current *societal values* such as those of the feminist movement ("this is a patriarchal society"). The meaning of other incidents might be related to the context of *professional values*, or of the *culture and values* of the project or organization.

Examples

A leading article in a newspaper illustrates how a journalist saw the meaning of the overthrow of Mr. Rutskoi by Mr. Yeltsin, in Russia in 1993, in relation to four embedded contexts:

> There are at least four levels to the drama. The most conspicuous is the personal struggle between Mr Yeltsin and his parliamentary opposition [interpersonal episode]. One level down is the clash of political principle between executive and legislature over what Mr Yeltsin has done [organizational values]. . . . The third level of the struggle is about job prospects in the new Russia [societal values]. . . . On the fourth level, down in the shifting subsoil of Russian history, is the more ancient struggle between Westernisers and Slavophiles over the identity and destiny of Russia itself [national values]. [*The Independent*, 4 October 1993]

In any pair or group in an organization, different contexts of meaning are likely to have the strongest influence for different people, so that incongruent meanings are attributed to the same speech act or interpersonal episode. Until meanings are negotiated, and myths are exploded or accepted, dysfunctional patterns of communication are very likely.

Questioning may need to move up the contextual hierarchy to explain what is complained about in terms of interpersonal episodes. The work with Ella we described above turned out over time to be a good example of this. The problem that Ella presented was a conflictual relationship with a co-worker in a group project, the co-worker coming from another team. Ella thought they were just incompatible because of their different views. It turned out that her co-worker's team were tending to look down on the team she belonged to. Only by discovering how easy it was to sort out the interpersonal conflict about running the group did Ella discover that there was a deeper problem, experienced in the pain of belonging to a team that was failing in its special mission (organizational values). Why were staff persisting in trying to bring about a change for which they had not the resources, the training, nor, for most of them, the motivation? What prevented them from reviewing the situation and correcting it? This was surmised to be a professional story of certain key senior managers. The situation had to be tackled at that level before the team would be allowed to change its mission. But because of their history, assumptions were made about staff in that team—that they were incompetent. So it is easy to see why a conflict might develop between two workers if one of them shares the myth that the other is part of an incompetent team.

Another example may resonate with the reader's experience. One of us [BP] was running a training course with a colleague, for established and aspiring training officers in a public sector organization. We encountered unexpected resistance to the way we were working, and eventually, in a tense review session, we discovered that many participants were preoccupied with what they had to do to gain the accreditation to which the course led. For us, the meaning of the sessions was derived from the "professional values" frame: we were helping the participants to fulfil a wish to be better trainers. For them, the meaning was derived from the "organizational values" frame: they were expecting severe job losses in the near future and wanted to secure their future by gaining more qualifications.

The context may be determined as much by *how* things are done, as by *what* is done. For example, in one organization the views of middle managers and workers about new directions were always elicited, respected, and taken into account and everyone knew that. Trouble arose only when this context was distorted by ambiguity. The director of the organization made a decision to develop certain new project work, with financing from the centre to ensure and control the development. Middle managers were consulted but felt that they had to agree even though they had reservations about the projects. The usual context of respect and listening was not clearly established. Over time it became apparent that these projects were somehow not "owned" in the same way as others by the managers who had to oversee them. There was uncertainty about their phasing and about whether they would develop to independence or be closed, in a way that was not the case elsewhere in the organization. This led to low staff morale and in-fighting among the project staff, which became time-consuming and worrying for the managers. The disagreements between management levels were not able to be surfaced and worked on. As a result the middle managers held a different organizational story and beliefs to the director.

Questioning beliefs

The following questions might be useful in opening up beliefs and meanings at different levels:

- Who shares the same views about policy, about ideologies, and about the need for change? Does someone in the relevant group lose out? Who agrees most with whom, and least with whom? What leads the actors to hold these beliefs? Where have they come from?

- On what overt principles is the team's work based? Are there clashes in values? Are there unclear or untested assumptions? Do practicalities really represent the values that the team may have agreed to adopt on an intellectual basis? Have the members enacted changes in practice that truly reflect the values set down in mission statements?

EXPLORING COVERT RULES

Belief systems and rules are of course connected. A manager was surprised when asked: "What is the rule in this team about staff meetings—if there is a rule?" She replied, ruefully: "Half the team arrive late and breathless and the other half have negotiated to leave early." One begins to hypothesize that this team feels that face-to-face communication is useless or dangerous. The surprise comes when the manager realizes that this hypothesis was staring her in the face. Because of the feelings engendered in her by the lack of respect for team meetings, and personal feelings of incompetence, she had evaded confronting the team and lost the opportunity to improve the meetings. Taking a systemic perspective is more than half way to tackling difficulties.

EXPLORING THE TIME DIMENSION

Consultants can often help managers and teams to reframe the current situation by exploring how the meaning they ascribe to it is related to past or imagined future contexts. Thus the life script of many social workers who later become managers is formed by their professional development, as well as by other events in their lives. Their practice as managers may be based on beliefs that are not relevant to their present task. They behave towards subordinates as if they were in a client relationship rather than a managerial one. They become preoccupied with the inner world of the subordinate, instead of clarifying the behaviour expected of them.

Conversely, the staff of training colleges can become so preoccupied with the future roles of their trainees that they are insensitive to the difficulties that the trainees have in living and working in their *present* context, which is the college or seminary. This is particularly stressful for mature adults who return to full-time education and find themselves treated as though they were eighteen-year-old students.

TYPES OF QUESTIONING

Comparative questioning

We have found it useful to press managers to translate broad generalizations into precise differences. For example, a manager might say that the department was in favour of a current reorganization. Instead of taking for granted that everyone was for this change, we would ask the manager to be more specific:

1. List the key people involved in managing this change.

2. On a scale of 0 (least) to 10 (most), where would you place each manager as regards being in favour of the change?

Clive, the senior manager we discussed in chapter one, concluded when he thought about this second point that only he and a
newish director were really wholeheartedly behind change; others
believed they would be disadvantaged or were not sufficiently
aware of the potential advantages. When he initially presented his
worry about why there were so many obstacles to progress, he had
thought that all his colleagues would be behind the director. This
question, which highlighted the costs and gains of change for different people, brought to the fore information that he had not wished
to focus on. Senior managers sometimes behave as though they
were unaware of the difference between changing an organization
in theory—which for some is a relatively painless effort—and actually changing one's day-to-day *actions* as those lower down the
hierarchy would have to do—which is a different and more difficult
process. Naturally, people in the organization will find all kinds of
ways to put a brake on changes that they do not understand. With
managers contemplating making organizational changes, it is useful
to ask questions like:

• Name the groups who will be most affected by the change. How
  will each group see themselves advantaged and disadvantaged
  by it?

Through these comparative questions we are asking clients to
make distinctions that were not apparent in their original story. If
this leads them to make new distinctions, they are beginning to
reframe or recreate the problem situation. Such questions can thus
be an intervention in themselves.

Circular questioning

We have already referred to our interest in the Milan method
(Selvini-Palazzoli, Boscolo, Cecchin, & Prata, 1978; Tomm, 1985),
which is a way of thinking about and acting in social systems,
used first in family therapy. Selvini-Palazzoli and her colleagues'
approach to questioning is influenced by their view of how systems
change:

> Systems continuously evolve because their "structure" is reflex-
> ively tied to "action". The family must act and whatever actions

they produce both "express" and reconstitute the structure of the system.

But not always in desirable directions! This is because families have to change as children grow up. In a different way so do organizations, as their staff and consumers or users change.

Systemic family therapists were much influenced by a seminal paper produced by the Milan Group (Selvini-Palazzoli et al., 1980) outlining the three principles they adopt in their work—hypothesizing, circularity, and neutrality. These principles can also, we think, be applied to work with teams, and with other groups who work together and have a history.

We will discuss hypothesizing fully in the following chapter. *Neutrality* can be interpreted to mean not so much a passive non-taking of sides as a positive taking of everyone's side in the quest the for understanding of how to intervene. This has been further developed by Cecchin (1987, p. 407), who describes neutrality as "a state of curiosity in the mind of the therapist. Curiosity leads to exploration and the invention of alternative views and moves and [these] breed curiosity" and keep the therapeutic team together.

Circularity describes the capacity of the consultant to conduct his or her investigation on the basis of feedback from the team, in response to the information solicited about relationships, difference, and change. As in family therapy, each member of the team in turn is asked to say how they see the relationship between two other members:

> By formally inviting one member of the family [team] to metacommunicate about the relationship of two others *in their presence*, we are not only breaking one of the ubiquitous rules of dysfunctional families, but we are also conforming to the first axiom of the pragmatics of human communication: . . . the various participants, try as they might, cannot avoid communicating. [Selvini-Palazzoli et al., 1980, p. 8]

Cecchin refers to the importance of an orientation towards understanding (in Bateson's phrase) "the pattern that connects", and towards the possibility of multiple patterns of causation. He says: "As long as there is a plurality of alternatives we are able to maintain a stance of curiosity" (Cecchin, 1987, p.. 407). Single descriptions of cause and effect tend to shut off further discussion. Curiosity is involving for the clients as well as the consultants!

Reflexive Questioning

Karl Tomm, who has closely studied the work of the Milan group and of Maturana, has introduced the concept of reflexive questioning; that is, of questions that not only unfold deeper meanings but also act as interventions because they invite reframing of behaviour or attitudes:

> Reflexive questions are questions asked with the intent to facilitate the self healing in an individual or family, by activitating the reflexivity among meanings within pre-existing belief systems that enables family members to generate constructive patterns of cognition and behaviour on their own. [1988]

Tomm categorizes the types of questioning he uses in his work as a therapist. We have found the following to be useful (see also Tomm, 1985).

1. *Observer perspective questions* can be used to draw out consequences, patternings of behaviour that the members may not yet be aware of. They can include questions about self-awareness and may also be directed towards increasing sensitivity to others.

The manager we have called Thomas, whom we mentioned briefly at the beginning of this chapter, asked why his organization left him free to do his own thing but simultaneously served to block him. This formulation puzzled the consultant group. They decided to offer him a hypothesis: he had difficulty because of his own ambivalence about his role and was therefore unable to change anything. Following this he revised his problem focus into a more pragmatic "How can I change my job and what to?" As part of the exploration he was asked:

- How would your line manager see your future—if he were here what would he say about his predictions of your career?

- Whom do you most admire—who are your heroes—whom would you most like to be like?

- How would key people in your personal life script your future—
  your wife, your mother, your father?

This exploration revealed to Thomas that his life script reflected diametrically opposed desires. Should he after all become an entrepreneur and even take on the family business as his father wished, or should he continue to work at his profession as his mother preferred?

2. *Unexpected context change questions* hinge on the fact that, whenever we ascribe a quality to something, we imply a contrast with an opposite or complementary quality. For example, a client who refers to someone as incompetent implies some standard of competence. If a project is described as a success, the speaker must have some notion of what is failure. If a management team is said to be confused, this implies a concept of clarity. Often it is unclear what implied comparisons a client is making. This type of question invites the speaker to make these implied distinctions explicit, by asking him or her to imagine circumstances in which the opposite quality was manifest. So, for example, when a manager calls a colleague's work incompetent, we might ask what this colleague is doing when he or she is experienced as competent? Or if the manager says that morale is low in the department, we might ask how things are different when morale is good.

3. *Future-oriented questions* are an attempt to bring into view feared or hoped-for images of the future that are influencing the manager's present behaviour. Often these are ill-defined images of dire catastrophe or of triumph and delight. So we might ask:

- What would it be like if the present conflict were resolved? What would the process by which it was resolved be like? What would be described as a typical success of the team in a year's time?

- If we fail to bring about any improvement in the situation you have described, what will be happening in a year's time? . . . And what would that lead to? . . . And why would that be so bad?

Like comparative questions, these questions oriented towards the future invite the manager to make new distinctions and thus recreate the reality he or she has to deal with. They also help managers and teams re-vision a future that has become cloudy and discover a fresh purpose or clarified aim to work towards. They can reveal that everyone in the team wishes the relations to be different, which is a good starting point for collaboration in change.

4. *Process interruption questions* are questions asked when something is actually going on in the presence of the consultant, which may be an accepted part of the team's way of doing things that no one notices any more, and which the consultant sees as a manifestation of the problem in hand. So, if an argument develops and is then abandoned, the consultant listens carefully to learn how the team deals with conflict. He or she may then interrupt the evasion process by asking questions such as:

- When you disagree, who usually wins and who loses?
- What would you say were the norms about disagreeing in this team?

This could be an important team learning experience, as they may not be aware of their evasion tactics. Or, as another example, a consultant might draw attention to a lack of finishing in a team that has trouble making decisions, by asking:

- Who would actually lose or gain most if you were to make a decision about this?

PIG IN THE MIDDLE

We have found that many of the problematic situations that managers have consulted us about on our workshops turn out to be connected with organizational change. Perhaps the title of the workshop, *Change Without Chaos?*, may have attracted managers preoccupied with large-scale disruption. As we have seen, if senior managers in an organization want rapid change because of a change in their values or prestige, or just natural impatience, there are usually others who fear that the rapid change would be too disruptive or risky, might lose money for the company, or might cause staff to leave. They will slow down the pace by various methods, including incompetent implementation of the new structures and procedures.

* * *

One manager who consulted us, Paula, was a newish head of a residential project for young people with handicaps. She was committed to putting into practice a change in philosophy that would result in parents coming into the residence and sharing care with staff. Staff were resisting this in subtle ways. Questioning brought out that the idea for the change had come from the last head, now promoted to be Paula's line manager. Paula felt in the middle between her manager's impatience for the change and her staff's resistance.

We asked about the potential gains and losses for the different groups involved and discovered that some staff feared that they would lose their jobs if parents took over their roles. These staff were, not surprisingly, resistant to change. It was not clear whether the new strategy would involve job losses or not. The previous project leader had been a visionary but had ignored the needs of staff. Staff were now making sure their needs would have to be focused on.

By asking the right questions the consultants had helped this head to feel more understanding of her staff and less anxious or uncertain about her own competence. She saw at once what she might do to reduce the uncertainties of the process for the staff, and proposed to involve both the personnel department and the trades union in the discussions.

CHAPTER FOUR

Constructing hypotheses

We all know the metaphor of being able to "step back"
far enough from the details "to see the forest for the
trees". But unfortunately for most of us, when we step
back we just see lots of trees. . . .

Senge, 1990, p. 127

Kate, when she had digested . . . all the good news in
The New York Times, decided to review her facts. It's not
the facts, it's the narrative they're arranged to tell, she
reminded herself.

Amanda Cross, 1990, p. 117

INTRODUCTION

We have discussed how we can use skilful questioning to
open up a situation described by a manager. One of the
purposes of such questioning is to enable us to formulate hypotheses about what is going on.

Hypothesizing is a dangerous word, because it comes out of a box labelled "science" and can lure us into supposing that managers and consultants live in a world of unambiguous facts, and of explanations that can be proved and disproved. As we see it, it is not as simple as that: we deal with selective descriptions of complex affairs by complex men and women—with stories, not facts. We are not therefore looking for the truth (the Truth!) about a situation, but rather—more modestly—for provisional and partial explanations that are *illuminating*, in that they suggest new meanings, and *useful*, in that they unparalyse people so that they can move on.

The word "hypothesis" comes from a Greek word that means a base or foundation—the same idea as that implied when we talk about the *underlying* causes of a problem. A hypothesis explains what is going on in terms of underlying factors or processes. A conjuror produces a tennis ball out of a stooge's ear. A child in the audience whispers to his mother: "He had it up his sleeve." In consultancy, hypotheses are seldom as tidy as this. Hypothesizing entails creating what seems to be a significant story from a mass of detail, and then proposing a mechanism that explains these events.

Re-telling

In our workshops we found that when we asked those participants acting as consultants to work out and offer hypotheses about the situation that had been described, they (and we) were seldom able to get there in one jump. Usually they began by re-telling what they had heard and understood. Sometimes this "re-telling" (we have borrowed this term from a literary academic, David Bleich: cf. Bleich, 1978) included a significant element of interpretation. Sometimes it was little more than a summary of what the presenter had said; but even then they had introduced something new by highlighting some elements in the presentation and ignoring others. In either case, in effect they reformulated the problem presented to them, in a way that the presenter either confirmed or found inadequate and modified.

Usually the consultants got no further than that; however, occasionally they went on to identify what they saw to be the process or mechanism driving the pattern of interactions they had described.

This seems to be a good way of approaching hypothesizing:

1. first, re-tell what you have heard in the form of a description that reformulates the problem;

2. then, explain the events you have described, and in particular the behaviour and perplexities of the manager, in terms of a credible process or mechanism.

At this second stage it helps to have some theories that suggest what a credible explanation might look like. We shall talk about this later.

* * *

Here is an example of a hypothesizing process that did not get beyond the re-telling stage. In one of our workshops a senior probation officer, Maureen, described an impasse she had reached in her work. She had to decide whether to provide a favourable reference for a social work student who had been in her team, whom she regarded as racist and unsuitable for accreditation. The student's present team leader and the training officer were both putting pressure on her to give the student a favourable reference. Maureen believed that the student might take out a grievance against her if she did not do so. Maureen had destroyed the records on which her assessment was based, when the student left her team.

After we had questioned Maureen (and drawn out more information than we have given here) we proceeded to the hypothesizing stage, and one of us put forward this statement:

Anti-racism in the organization is taken seriously only in rhetoric. There are not enough black staff in post to make white people feel uncomfortable. Maureen fears she may become a sacrifice for a crunch issue, if she insists on acting according to the spirit of the anti-racist policy. She is paralysed by the lack of support for the policy.

There is a clear element of interpretation in this statement. Maureen's inability to decide what to do is explained by means of a metaphor—she is afraid of becoming a *sacrifice*—and by placing this particular incident in the context of the organization as a whole. It proposes that the organization's policy is largely rhetoric: when people are faced with acting upon the policy, they pick up signals indicating that they will not be supported.

This is a sharp re-telling, and the beginnings of a hypothesis. It suggests that anyone else who wanted to draw attention to racist practices would face a similar dilemma, and if the presenter responded by telling us about someone else who had, say, backed down after making an allegation of racism, we might become more committed to it. But it is incomplete as a hypothesis, in that it does not state how Maureen herself is contributing to the dilemma she describes. She is depicted as a victim ("sacrifice", "paralysed") rather than as an agent. If she is to identify some real choices for herself, and cease to be immobilized between impossible alternatives, she will need to understand what she is already doing, and why.

We were unable to reach a complete hypothesis during the workshop. Later in this chapter we give an example of a consultation that clearly moved into the second stage of hypothesizing.

WHAT IS A HYPOTHESIS?

Maturana and Varela (1987, p. 28) provide a precise definition of a hypothesis. It is: "a conceptual system capable of generating the phenomenon to be explained in a way acceptable to a body of observers."

They are saying that a hypothesis suggests a model or mechanism ("a conceptual system") by which the observable problematic events are brought about. They go on to say that a useful hypothesis also predicts or draws attention to other phenomena not included in the original description. The explanation also has to be convincing to somebody: the hypothesis of a ball up the conjuror's sleeve would be more persuasive to us than that of a ball inside the stooge's head. Our first-draft hypothesis about Maureen's impasse is credible if we can accept that publicly declared policies often conceal variable commitment, and that this might lead to an individual feeling paralysed.

Hypothesizing is not a specialized skill; it is part of everyday life. We could not function if we did not construct hypotheses to explain unforeseen events. Forming hypotheses enables us to act. The problem for managers, as for everybody else, is that there are some situations in which we are unable to explain what is going on; or, more frequently, in which our hypotheses have the force of certainty for us but do not enable us to act in a constructive way. There seem to be no alternatives except to resign or shoot somebody.

The challenge of systems thinking is that we should make our hypotheses explicit (rather than working on unexpressed assumptions) and testable (in the sense that they suggest questions or actions that will support them or call them into question). It requires that we recognize the difference between linear, cause-and-effect, hypotheses and circular hypotheses, which map out patterns of interaction that perpetuate stuck situations. And it requires that we sit loose by our hypotheses, rather than becoming wedded to them as true and complete explanations, recognizing that they are our creations in words and symbols and can never embrace the complexity of the situation itself.

HYPOTHESIZING AND CURIOSITY

Most of us have been educated to expect that problems will have single, correct solutions. In our workshops we have found that people find it more useful and indeed liberating to be offered several hypotheses, which may be unconnected or even contradictory. Irrespective of what the hypotheses are, the fact that a group of people can have so many different responses to the same story shows that the meaning of the situation cannot be as obvious as the presenter supposed. Once we become committed to one explanation of something, we cease to be curious about it. Cecchin (1987) has suggested that hypothesizing is intimately connected with curiosity: "Curiosity is a stance, whereas hypothesizing is what we do to try to maintain this stance" (p. 411).

In order to be able to think creatively about a situation and so frame new hypotheses about it, it is necessary to get into a frame of mind that Cecchin here calls curiosity. Other systemic writers talk about taking up a "meta" position. "Meta" is a prefix used in many words (metamorphosis, metabolism) and denotes a shift of some kind, in position or condition. In systems practice a "meta" position is one of being what Zen writers call "fully involved and unconcerned". In this frame of mind we are able to hypothesize, and working at hypothesizing enables us to sustain this frame of mind.

This explains why offering a manager one or preferably more hypotheses about her situation can be a potent intervention, whether or not it is translated into suggestions for action. Listening to the hypotheses gives her a new "meta" perspective on her difficulties, one in which she can have an involved and yet detached curiosity about them. This is what seems to have happened for Gillian (see chapter two), when she ceased to be overwhelmed by the problem of securing the future of her project. It may also have happened for another manager, after a consulting exercise we have not described, when she reported:

> I now have a different perspective on [my two teams]. I have come to see that I am not omnipotent. Going home I thought, "There is no way I can roll this stone about reviewing child care policy, in the midst of all this restructuring".

LINEAR AND CIRCULAR HYPOTHESES

We discussed in chapter one the distinction between linear and circular explanations of behaviour. In general terms, circular hypotheses explain the persistence of the problem behaviour in terms of *closed feedback loops*. They describe conditions of *homeostasis*, that is, of stable patterns that persist in spite of, or with the help of, efforts to change them ("homeostasis" is derived from two Greek words which mean "like-standing"). And they explain *how problem-owners perpetuate problems* by their own behaviour, like people who hate purring but go on stroking their cats.

Formulating a useful circular hypothesis entails adopting a position in which, like Hawkeye in M*A*S*H, we do not take sides. The hypothesis thus is not skewed by our blaming one of the parties or our wish that things should be otherwise—we have already quoted part of the following statement by Cecchin, in which he talks about *respecting* the system:

> Respecting a system means that you act towards a system with the recursive understanding that the system is simply doing what it does, and that this doing is the it that does it. [1987, p. 408]

When we began using systemic thinking we were primarily concerned with achieving the shift in our way of thinking which would enable us to "see" circular causality where previously we had seen only linear causality.

Faced with a situation we do not understand, our first hypotheses tend to be linear. Sometimes they are useful and we look no further. If a manager says he has a problem with a member of staff who is continually making mistakes, it may be enough to propose that the cause of the problem is the staff member's lack of competence in the necessary skills. Until this has been tested, say by providing training, there is little point in looking for greater complexity. If, however, we find that the manager is unwilling to consider providing training, or that the staff member is already competent to do the job, we may conclude that there is more in this than meets the eye, and that only a systemic, circular hypothesis will have the necessary leverage.

Even with manifestly complex problems, it is a good idea to hold on to any linear hypotheses we come up with, since they may form the building blocks of a circular hypothesis, as they did in the case of the woman stroking the cat.

We described earlier how Sarah, the leader of a community project, asked for advice about an uncooperative and disaffected team member, Robert, in her team: how could she help him to be an integral part of the project? This is part of the hypothesis offered by one of the group:

> Robert is disaffected, doesn't share the aims of the project leader. Perhaps he wanted the project leader's job, [feels he has] lost status, has hurt his self-image. There is an issue about his actual intellectual ability. . . .

This was a relevant re-telling of Robert's possible state of mind, and it amounts to a linear hypothesis. The group member attributes Sarah's problem with Robert to Robert's state of mind and intellectual ability. On its own this hypothesis was unlikely to be useful to Sarah. What it does not say is what she or other people in the team and beyond are doing to activate Robert's feeling of disaffection, or to make him aware of his intellectual limitations. Elaboration such as this would not have discounted the linear hypothesis; rather, it would have incorporated it in a circular one.

There is no one correct way of constructing a hypothesis. We have gradually built up a repertoire of hypothesis shapes, in the way one builds up a repertoire of chess openings one can play, or meals one can cook. There is no short cut to discovering which ones are useful.

POSITIVE FEEDBACK AND SCHISMOGENESIS

A circular hypothesis is a representation of a system of interactions which in some way brings a repetitive pattern of communications or behaviour into view. Some forms of hypothesis refer explicitly to the feedback processes that constitute the pattern. (In chapter one we defined a system as *structured by feedback*.)

There are two kinds of feedback, positive and negative. Positive feedback leads to escalation, negative feedback to equilibrium. A familiar system structured by positive feedback is, sadly, that of two nations engaged in an arms race. Nation A fears that Nation B is ahead of them in their destructive capacity, so they increase the volume or sophistication of their arms production. News of this reaches Nation B, and arouses fear that Nation A may soon overtake them, so they in turn increase their production and development of new weapons; and so it goes on. The feedback is said to be positive because each bit of news amplifies the response of the one who receives it. A positive feedback loop is of the form shown in Diagram 5.

Watzlawick and his colleagues (1974, pp. 31ff) call this pattern the "more-of-the-same" solution. This is an attempt to solve a problem by repeating or stepping up a remedy that has so far not worked. Sometimes this is appropriate: one paracetamol does not relieve our headache, so we take another. But in many situations repeating an ineffective remedy only makes it worse, because it provokes more of the behaviour it was intended to change.

Diagram 5

Watzlawick gives the example of a wife who feels that her husband is concealing something from her, so she starts to question him and check up on what he has been doing. He finds this intrusive and becomes more secretive, even withholding harmless information "just to teach her a lesson". This further fuels her mistrust and anxiety, making her more persistent in probing for information. This leads him to conceal more; and so it goes on.

Bateson (1972) described two types of system based on positive feedback, which he called "symmetrical" and "complementary". An arms race is symmetrical: the more A produces arms, the more B produces arms. It is the logic of the song "Anything you can do, I can do better". A pathologically dependent relationship is complementary: the *more* A does for B, the *less* B does for himself. It is the logic of the "fatal attraction" love affair: A becomes increasingly demanding of B, to the point where B begins to back off. This makes A even more demanding, and eventually, in desperation, B tries to end the relationship, which only has the effect of causing A to pursue him or her even more relentlessly. Watzlawick's "more-of-the-same" example is of this form.

It will be apparent that these escalating processes cannot go on for ever: in the words of another song, "Something's gotta give". One possible outcome is what Bateson called "schismogenesis", which means "split-production". The process gives rise to a split, in which the system is destroyed: knowing it cannot match the other's arms production, one nation starts a war; unable to possess, or escape, the other person, one lover kills the other. Fighting between fans breaks out after a football match: the mutual defiance and taunting cannot be contained within the system of ritualized combat of the game, and real combat erupts.

Fortunately there are alternatives to schismogenesis. One is any kind of device, which is triggered when an unacceptable level of escalation has been reached, that intervenes to break the feedback loop. It is the equivalent of an electrical fuse, or of sprinklers installed against fire in a building. Wilfred Bion identifies something like this in *Experiences in Groups* (1961, p. 125). He describes a situation in which the members of a group are torn between the belief that their leader is a genius and the belief that he is mad. They swing between these two extreme views with increasing rapidity, until the group can no longer contain the emotional situation, which thereupon spreads with explosive violence to other groups, until enough groups have been drawn in to absorb the reaction. In practice in the small group [i.e. Bion's therapeutic groups at the Tavistock Clinic] this means impulsion to complain to outside authority, e.g. write to the press, or to a Member of Parliament, or the authorities of the Clinic. The object of this is . . . to bring in so much inert material, in the way of outsiders . . . who do not share the emotional situation, that the new and much larger group ceases to vibrate.

The other alternative is the mobilization of another process, often slower, which counteracts the effects of the positive feedback loop. If there were no such processes, it would be a dangerous business to start stroking a cat. In the case of an arms race, the depletion of the manufacturing resources of the two nations may provide this counteracting effect. The demand to produce more and better weapons increasingly overloads their industries, depletes stocks of raw materials, and exhausts the ingenuity of scientists. This seems to have been one of the factors that brought the race between the Soviet Union and the Unites States to an end.

Light can be thrown on many intractable organizational problems by hypotheses based on this pattern of escalating and counteracting loops. Peter Senge (1990, p. 379) and his collaborators have identified about a dozen distinct combinations of such loops which recur in organizational and social life. He calls these "systems archetypes". The pattern we have just discussed he calls the "Limits to Growth" archetype. The counteracting loop is an example of negative feedback, which we will now discuss.

NEGATIVE FEEDBACK

Negative feedback is feedback that corrects deviations from a normative state. Such mechanisms are familiar in everyday life. Physiological mechanisms maintain our body temperature at around 37°C: if we get too hot we sweat; if we get too cold we shiver. A cyclist corrects the bicycle's continuous tendency to fall over by making small turns of the handlebars to the right or the left; the cyclist senses the bicycle beginning to fall as negative feedback, and responds to it—unless he or she is a beginner—quite automatically.

Diagram 6

A significant part of the work of managers and administrators is concerned with setting goals and standards and correcting deviations from these norms. Stocks are getting low; we must buy more supplies. Reports to the committee are reaching them too close to the date of the meeting; we must produce them sooner. Party membership is declining; we must set up a campaign to recruit more members. So negative feedback loops are of the form presented in Diagram 6.

Senge (1990, pp. 89ff) has pointed out that there is often a delay before the effects of corrective action make themselves felt (see Diagram 7). If this delay is not recognized, there can be serious consequences. When the action we take seems to have no effect, we may think nothing is happening and intervene again, so that when the change works through we find that we have over-reacted. Senge gives the familiar example of a shower. The water is too cold, so we

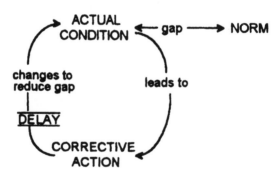

Diagram 7

turn the regulator in the direction of the red (hot) arrow. There is no immediate improvement in the temperature, so we turn the regulator again. Now the water begins to warm up, but because we have over-reacted it continues to get hotter until we have to jump out of the shower.

In the past few years, as the British economy has plunged into recession, many organizations have responded to a deteriorating cash position by laying off staff. Recently we have heard of more than one that has subsequently found itself having to re-engage some of the same staff on a contract basis and has been *able to pay them*. One manager said: "If only we had waited! We did not need to lay off so many." It appears that they were so anxious about financial viability that they could not wait for the first economies to make themselves felt, and went on cutting unnecessarily.

MORE COMPLEX FEEDBACK PATTERNS

Many organizational and societal processes are too complex to be modelled adequately by single positive or negative feedback loops. We have already indicated that processes that initially escalate and then level off can sometimes be represented by a pattern of positive and negative loops which Senge calls "Limits to Growth" (see Diagram 8; the plus and minus signs in the diagram indicate the positive and negative loops). The escalating action exacerbates the problematical condition. The corrective action diminishes it.

This is a familiar pattern. Many voluntary organizations, with a charismatic founder and enthusiastic workers, achieve amazing results in their early years. Later the rate of growth and achievement slows down or even goes into reverse, as the scale of the operation

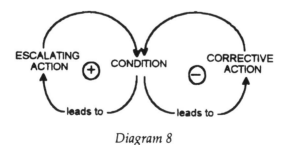

Diagram 8

requires more formal organization and professional management, and later generations of staff and volunteers are less willing to burn themselves out for the cause.

In chapter six we describe another of the feedback patterns identified by Senge.

Sometimes stuckness in an organization manifests itself as an *oscillation* between different positions, none of which is tenable. Such situations can sometimes be illuminatingly interpreted as manifestations of irresolvable *dilemmas* that are inherent in the way the organization or part of it is constituted in the minds of its members. We outline this powerful approach to hypothesizing in chapter six.

As we have said, there is no right way of formulating a hypothesis. The test of its adequacy is in its explanatory power, in providing an explanation of the problem situation, and in its usefulness in opening up new options for action. In this next section we set out a number of other approaches to systemic hypothesizing.

ARTICULATING RULES

A good way to get a handle on the repetitive patterns of behaviour in a team or organization is to describe them in terms of rules that people appear to be observing. There is no suggestion that they are aware of any rules themselves, or indeed that the rules exist anywhere but in the words that the consultant uses to articulate them. But they are useful if they enable the consultant or members of the client group to name, however crudely, what is going on.

For example, a consultant might notice that the client's story includes several similar sequences of events (we will imagine that the client is the director of a voluntary organization). On each occasion that the headquarters staff announced a new initiative, there was vociferous criticism from voluntary members in different parts of the country, leading to a row in the management board between the director and the trustees about curtailing the initiative. The sentence we have just written is already the beginnings of a hypothesis: it proposes that there is this repetition in the director's account. It could be formulated as a series of rules, like this:

Rule 1:   Every time the HQ staff take an initiative, the volunteers shall voice strong criticisms.

Rule 2:   Every time the volunteers voice criticisms of staff initiatives, there shall be a row in the management board between the director and the trustees.

This hypothesis has immediate usefulness, in that it gives rise to further questions. Do the volunteers object to every initiative, or only those connected with, say, fund-raising? Or only those initiated by a particular staff member? Do all volunteers object, or is there an identifiable sub-group? Are these the only rows in the management board, or are there others? These questions may lead to the framing of more focused rules, or to the conclusion that these supposed regularities are illusory.

Working with these essentially linear (A → B) rules may generate more information, which leads to the formulation of a circular or self-referential rule. For example:

The staff introduce a new procedure . . .

. . . so the volunteers protest . . .

. . . so there is a row in the board . . .

. . . so the director withdraws the procedure . . .

. . . so the staff introduce another procedure . . .

. . . and the volunteers object . . .

. . . and so on . . .

We have found that reflecting back to a group the rules they appear to be obeying—or better still, working with them to formulate the rules—can be an effective intervention. Once the rules have been named, it is difficult for the group to carry on exactly as they did before. Or there may be one more row in the board, and then someone says: "Here we go again!", and people begin to back off and look for another way of proceeding.

So the approach to hypothesizing based on formulating tacit rules for the team or organization can be seen as a way of constructing feedback loops, and also as a way of constructing an intervention.

NEW STORIES FOR OLD

It is also possible to describe the patterning of behaviour in an organization in the form of a repeating story. Like the approach through rules, this has the advantage of being easily communicable to members of the organization. In the consultation with Sarah (chapter three), one of us put forward this hypothesis:

> This is the story of a man who has great understanding of the young people, and for whom the new philosophy of the project makes no emotional sense. The more you pressure him, the more he takes evasive action (i.e. it is a "more-of-the-same" solution).

There is potential leverage in this hypothesis, in that it invites the client and the consultants to see the situation from the position of the worker rather than that of the project leader—as they had tended to do. It may also remind them of other situations in which an experienced worker has been sceptical of new organizational initiatives, when they may have identified with the worker; so it has emotional appeal. It also identifies the circularity and symmetry of the pattern that has been described: the more you push the worker, the more he pushes back.

There is more to working with stories than this. There is a developing approach to individual and family therapy, recently described by White and Epston (1990) and Gustafson (1992), that is beginning to be applied to organizational life. These writers suggest that describing family (or organizational) affairs in terms of stories is more than an interpretative device for consultants. In their view, our culture supplies us with a repertoire of stories of the life of an individual man, an individual woman, a marriage, a family, a work-group, or an organization. These condition what we expect to happen, and what we perceive to be happening. Consequently, we enact familiar dramas and are unable to create alternative trajectories for ourselves—new stories that are not in the cultural anthology.

In these terms, the purpose of a consultant may be construed as working with the client system to find a new story for itself. This is not a matter of trying to bring the old story to an end: focusing on it, even with the intention of ending it, only keeps it alive. It is, rather, a matter of exploring where another, preferred, story is already being enacted, unnoticed, and diverting energy into it. Cooper and Gustafson (1992) describe how the consultant seeks to "stay on the edge" between the old and new stories. There is a strong pull towards becoming enmeshed in the old story; there is also a danger of becoming over-identified with the new story and alienating those who are identified with the old. At the time of writing we have not had a lot of experience of working with this approach. But its value may prove to be that it enables consultants to take a long view and avoid expecting too much too quickly. They can observe and discuss how the old story continues to play itself out, and also how the new story reappears and develops new sub-plots. Insofar as they are able to stay on the edge in this way, they make it possible for members of the client system to extricate themselves as well.

REFRAMING

Underlying all the approaches to hypothesizing that we have described is a fundamental strategy, derived from family therapy, known as *reframing*. Watzlawick and colleagues define reframing in this way:

> To reframe means to change the conceptual or emotional setting or viewpoint in relation to which a situation is experienced, and to place it in another frame, which fits the "facts" of the same concrete situation equally well or even better, and thereby changes its entire meaning. [1974, p. 95]

Events have meaning for us according to the context in which we place them—or, in the terms we are using here, according to the way we frame them. A sunny day has one meaning for a family setting out on holiday, another for a farmer after weeks of drought, another for an environmentalist concerned about global warming. Or, in the words of the couplet:

> Two men looked through prison bars.
> One saw mud, the other stars.

The mythical story of the labours of Thor shows the effect of reframing an experience of failure. Thor is set a series of tasks by the gods. One is to drink a huge horn of wine. Thor raises the horn to his lips and drinks and drinks, but when he is full and exhausted he finds he has made little or no impression on it: it is still full to the brim. He believes he has failed the test and is amazed to find that the gods are full of admiration. It turns out that the horn contained the oceans of the world, and that his drinking created the tides, which continue to this day. He had *really* been making waves! It is a consoling story for those who take on huge problems and are disillusioned when they fail. In chapter one we described the multidisciplinary team, who "had seen themselves as failures, unable to live up to their ideal of teamliness", but who "began to see themselves as achieving a modest but useful level of collaboration in face of massive obstacles".

The concept of reframing has been elaborated by Cronen and Pearce in their theory of the Co-ordinated Management of Meaning, outlined here in chapter three. In that chapter, we described how a probation officer, Ella, discovered new ways of viewing and dealing with disagreements with an officer in another team, when a process of consultation enabled her to place this conflict in the context of differences and confusions at higher levels in her organizational hierarchy.

Before discovering ways of reframing a situation, it may be necessary for a manager to "de-frame" it—that is, to abstract it from its immediate context and the feelings that go with that, and to recover his or her curiosity about what is going on, for its own sake. When it is out of its frame, the manager may notice other things going on that were previously ignored because they did not fit the dominant story. He or she may have glimpses of other stories. Stuckness is often "stucker" because those involved can't see things that don't fit their disaster story. What are sometimes called "awaydays", when a team spends a day away from the office in a hotel, are a device for de-framing the affairs of the team. The potential for de-framing is further reinforced by the participation of an outside person, for whom the goings-on in the team are not episodes in a familiar story, and whose ignorance requires those involved to look again at, and describe, events whose meaning they had taken for granted.

POSITIVE CONNOTATION

Positive connotation is a particular form of reframing, in which behaviour that has been presented as bad is reframed as—within a particular frame of reference—functional, and therefore in that sense good. In chapter one we described a situation presented by a social services manager, Clive, whose attempts to implement changes in the department were being impeded by an uncooperative team member. It was discovered that the changes were not popular with some managers in the department. The consulting group suggested that

> . . . one way of reading this situation was that they were *preventing the Department from moving too fast*. His uncooperative team member might represent a sizeable body of people who wanted to hold on to what was tried and familiar in their way of working.

The positive connotation implied by this hypothesis is clearest in the words we have italicized. This kind of reframing implies a supposition that, whatever is happening in an organization, it is the best way that those involved have been able to evolve so far of finding a way through the conflicting wishes and instructions they have to live with. It is a strategy for treating the system with respect, even when the consultant feels the pull of the client's negative feelings.

WORKING WITH HYPOTHESES

It is one thing to be able to formulate a systemic hypothesis, and another to be able to use it. In the next chapter we consider ways of translating hypotheses into options for action. Prior to that, however, is the question of to whom the hypothesis is addressed. If we regard the one acting as consultant as the speaker, who is the listener? The listener may be the consultant himself or herself, the manager presenting the problem to the consultant, or the group of people who are implicated in the problem—the people who figure in the manager's story, the client system. We will examine each of these possibilities in turn, in reverse order.

Addressing the client system

In our workshops we have found that managers often assume that the best way to use hypotheses that they have found illuminating is to pass them on to their team or other people in their organization. They have convened meetings to pass on "what I was told on this course" and hung up diagrams behind their office door. A report by Mark, whose story we discuss in a chapter six, illustrates the difficulty of assessing how wise this is. At a workshop he had been given a hypothesis in diagrammatic form. He said:

> I used the diagram as a training aid in seminars and in a departmental meeting. There was a mixed reaction, from black and white staff: some found it interesting, some beyond their understanding.

If it makes no sense it is of no help, but an initially incomprehensible statement can be potent if the listeners go on worrying away at it. It seems more promising if the listeners find it interesting, but is it? Archimedes, who first formulated the hypothesis known as Archimedes' Principle, found it more than interesting when he got into the bath and the water overflowed. According to the writer Vitruvius:

> When the idea flashed across his mind, the philosopher jumped out of the bath exclaiming "Eureka! Eureka!" and, without waiting to dress himself, ran home to try the experiment. ["Eureka", in *Brewer's Dictionary*, 1981]

The question is not whether the listeners find the hypothesis interesting, but whether they want to *engage* with the hypothesis— to "try the experiment"—and their desire to do this can be too naively assumed.

There may be several problems involved in passing on a hypothesis to a group of colleagues. The manager may in so doing avoid engaging with the hypothesis himself (or herself). He may arouse antagonism in the group by indicating that he has been discussing their affairs with strangers and is now, in effect, introducing the strangers into their midst in the form of their ideas. He may ignore the possibility that the hypothesis will, if it is any good, arouse resistance amongst those for whom the existing stuck situation provides practical and emotional gains—which it must if they are so strongly committed to it.

Addressing the client

Consultation is often unstressful as long as the consultant and the client sit side by side and analyse a problem "over there", as it were. In our workshops many of the hypotheses offered to presenters do not include the presenter in the hypothesis. For example, a team leader presented the problem of a stuck worker in the team: how could this worker be helped to move on in a positive way? A pair of workshop members offered this hypothesis:

> Because she has always been out on a limb, separate from the rest of the team, and because of the reputation that she has developed (rightly or wrongly), she is now fulfilling an essential team function—that of knocking the board. (If you took her away, someone else would take her place.)

This is an implicitly circular hypothesis, in that it implies that the worker and the rest of the team are linked in a system in which she plays an essential role. But the team leader is not included in the system: the leader is represented as someone who can intervene from outside but will not disturb the pattern.

Another consultant pair included the team leader in their hypothesis, and they suggested that she might be part of the problem:

> This person represents some underlying anxiety within the team—possibly around job security related to funding—and provides a smoke screen. [The team leader] has been drawn into protecting and siding with the individual, which may only serve to increase the antagonism of the rest of the team towards the individual and therefore increase her defensiveness.

Consultants require more finesse at the point where they want to offer hypotheses in which the presenter is part of the problem, either (as here) through their behaviour in the feedback system which has come into view, or through the way they are framing the situation they describe. Those just quoted temper the wind to the shorn lamb by representing the leader as having been passively "drawn in", with unfortunate consequences. A sharper hypothesis would have explained what the team leader gained from directing the antagonism of the team at the stuck worker by protecting and siding with her.

Looking for trouble

A transcript of another consultation shows how a team leader, Hugh, and a consultant group arrived at a reading of a difficult situation which did include the satisfaction that Hugh was gaining from it. Hugh described how he had accepted an invitation from his senior management team to lead a new specialist team, whose members would be drawn from three other teams in the locality. The team was created without consultation with the staff concerned, and the idea was resisted by the leaders and members of the three teams. After a period of questioning the group put forward re-tellings of his story. This is Hugh's own re-telling of his initially much longer presentation:

> Hugh has had no role in creating this team. The majority of his new team, and also the team leaders he will have to work with and the three remaining community teams, are lukewarm about the idea to say the least. He is therefore rather isolated and feels that the whole weight of making this team work falls on him.

The consultants (C1, C2) wondered why Hugh had accepted the job:

C1: So why did you sign on for this?

H: Because it was new. Because I like starting things from scratch, to a non-established pattern. It was naive enthusiasm, but I'm stimulated by change.

He must have gone on thinking about this question, because later he returned to it:

H: About my motivation: both the two previous management jobs I've had have been in terrible situations. One was a hostel in which the previous warden had messed things up, and the other was a scheme in which the previous manager had been sacked. I hadn't made this connection: I seem to be attracted to situations of extreme difficulty.

C2: Were you ever in the parachute corps?

C1: If we went on to interventions now we could congratulate you . . .

H: . . . On doing the same again. Yes.

C1: You've found the kind of work you really like!

Addressing oneself

Sometimes a hypothesis is best taken as addressed to oneself as the consultant. This is of course what is intended when a manager takes time out to analyse his or her own situation, alone. But a hypothesis that leads to change frequently does so by prising us as consultants away from assumptions and identifications that are coupling us too strongly into the feedback loops we are trying to unravel. (We talk about a consultant being "outside" the problem situation, but there are no insides and outsides in this kind of systems thinking. Feedback loops are no respecters of conventional boundaries.)

Consultants, like the team leaders in the previous two illustrations, bring their own conscious and unconscious desires to their work. Their capacity to frame hypotheses, and so generate new meanings, is constrained by their own identifications, most importantly with theories and ideologies. The Filofax of one of the writers offers a wise thought for each week. For one week while we were writing this book, it said:

There are no stumbling-blocks save in the spirit.

This adherence to their own identifications is concealed or alleviated in our workshops by the fact that the participants act as a group of consultants and offer several hypotheses. The plurality and often diversity of the hypotheses makes it clear that none of them has a claim on the whole truth. Nevertheless, one can sometimes see that the group is restricted in the scope of its hypothesizing by shared beliefs in social work values, or democratic values, or a belief in unconscious group processes or systems theory. Every theory and value system is like a torch in a dark room: it illuminates things that were previously obscure, and it also leaves in darkness the things it does not pick up.

Looking for trouble (continued)

To illustrate some of the aspects of hypothesizing we have discussed in this chapter, we will continue the account of the consultation with Hugh (the team leader from the parachute corps!).

After the interchange we have reported, Hugh continued to re-spond to the re-tellings. In the course of this he expanded the frame in which he had described the situation, which triggered a new line of thinking from one of the group:

> H: This was stimulated from outside the organization by the government. So there was a change in the requirements of the outside world, to which the organization had got to respond in some way. And they chose to respond in this particular way.

> C2: This raises an interesting point of systems thinking. Once the senior management themselves experience imposed change, they tend to act coherently with the reality they've just experienced. So they impose change. This organization is part of a culture in this country now of always being on the receiving end of imposed change, and it is altering management styles and values.

This observation led us into the hypothesizing phase. Members of the group worked in pairs to produce statements. The first pair said:

> The management of this organization react to a legal requirement without advanced planning and consultation, even though this was on the cards for some time. They react by turning to talented individuals to try to dump on them the responsibility to carry out the legal requirements. Hugh is one of these talented individuals, who enjoys change and is apparently good at handling difficult situations. The more successful he is at handling this situation, the more it confirms senior management in this way of operating. Hugh also gets the reward of doing what he likes doing, and also presumably gets senior management approval for it. So senior management continue to act in this sort of fashion, not in a properly thought-out collaborative way.

This hypothesis proposes an organizational story in which a senior management group, who have got scope to protect the organization from the effects of imposed change, are rescued from the potentially damaging consequences of imposing change themselves, by "talented individuals" who make the changes work. The circularity of the hypothesis is clear: the more the talented individuals rescue their senior managers, the more the senior managers introduce change without consultation, and so the more the talented individuals have to rescue them.

The hypothesis is framed by a value system that places a negative connotation on the behaviour of senior management: they "dump" responsibility, they do not act in a "properly thought-out collaborative way". Hugh is correspondingly idealized: he is "talented", is "apparently good at handling difficult situations". We can see this bias in the story as the means by which the consultants protect their relationship with their client, Hugh. It illustrates our earlier point about the way consultants' capacities to generate new meanings are constrained by their own identifications and ideologies. If the consultants had been able to recognize and bracket out their own feelings about the situation, they might have congratulated the senior management *in absentia* on the skilful way in which they were using their staff to get government directives implemented, without spending valuable time and energy on planning and consultation. This might have presented Hugh more starkly with the way, as they saw it, he was collaborating with this strategy.

The second pair of consultants said:

Hugh's original interpretation, that his skills are entirely relevant to the creation of this new team, has given way to misgivings that are in danger of becoming self-fulfilling. The senior management failings and the consequent resistance [in the organization] are fuelling this. So Hugh's original frame—a positive identification of the new concept and his ability to carry it out successfully—is being undermined.

We asked them whether they saw this as a linear or a circular hypothesis (the reader may like to consider the same question). It turned out that the key word in the hypothesis was "fuelling". They were trying to describe an escalating spiral of demoralization: Hugh is initially enthusiastic, but he is demoralized by the anger about the imposed changes in the organization. The undermining of Hugh's enthusiasm further fuels the negativity in the organization, which

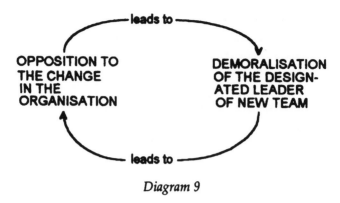

Diagram 9

gets to him even more ... From the point of view of consultant technique, this hypothesis might have been expressed more clearly as in Diagram 9.

The third hypothesis was:

Hugh is protecting the mainstream work of the organization against government intervention, by putting himself forward as willing to lead a team out of the organization into government service, at the cost of his credibility as a change agent for the organization.

It left Hugh and the group with baffled looks, perhaps because there had been no suggestion that Hugh would take his team out of the organization. One of the pair who produced it explained that "by definition, as identities build up with other people in similar work, you belong to another system altogether". This is another version of our statement earlier in this chapter that feedback loops are no respecters of conventional boundaries. This led the analysis into a new area, in which Hugh articulated how he saw himself as reinventing the practice of the organization in a way that was compatible with its present political environment. One indicator of a useful hypothesis is that it leads the client to reframe his situation. The episode reminds us that it is a mistake to assume that a hypothesis will do its work without explanation or discussion. Often it will require patient working through. The most important thing about the initial formulation is that the consultants have said something new *to themselves*.

CHAPTER FIVE

Finding a new course

> "The question is", said Humpty Dumpty, "which is to be master—that's all."
>
> Lewis Carroll, *Through the Looking Glass*

The purpose of an intervention is, first, to provide a means of communicating the meaning of a hypothesis to the client; second, to provide a means of testing its usefulness; and third, of course, to nudge the client system into moving on and finding a new course. In our workshops, interventions can also be a tactful way of saying: "You are expected to do something different, as well as perceive something different, about this situation."

As we outlined in chapters three and four, asking questions and offering hypotheses are themselves interventions, when they lead the manager to reframe his or her problem situation. People do not necessarily *decide* to act on new information: they may spontaneously change their behaviour because their reality has changed.

Until very recently there was less theory to guide interventions than the theories that supported the domains of exploring and explaining. Recent management and organization development texts are beginning to flesh out the bones of systemic interventions in organizations (Wynne, L.C., 1986; Hampden-Turner, 1990; Senge 1990; Campbell, Draper, & Huffington, 1991b; Torbert, 1991).

PARADOX

Living is essentially paradoxical to the systems theorist. In their seminal text on family therapy, Selvini-Palazzoli and her collaborators (1978) point out that as human beings we have to find a way between two modes of communication: through verbal language, which is essentially linear in structure, and through the non-verbal language of behaviour, which is essentially circular, based on feedback. Verbal language is structured grammatically around subject and object, and it creates a "before" and an "after" in the sense of who performs and who receives an action: "this implies cause and effect and in consequence a moralistic definition" (p. 53). But what is communicated through behaviour and action is recursive—analogical rather than digital. Human beings and social systems must change constantly in order to survive, but language creates an illusion of conservatism and stability. So we are led to fear change and deny our capacity to change, although in fact we are changing all the time as a biological and social necessity. In rigidly controlled families presenting a schizophrenic member, every change is seen as a threat, and the system reacts with increasing rigidity.

> These families and systems sustain their "game" through an intricacy of paradoxes which can only be undone by counter paradoxes in the context of therapy. [Selvini-Palazzoli et al., 1978, p. 8]

Systems practice is therefore, from one point of view, a struggle with language, and the question is, as Humpty Dumpty says, who is to be master.

One famous example of a paradoxical communication is the injunction: "I am your parent: you ought to love me." Love, however, is a spontaneous and freely given emotion, and cannot be commanded; it is quite different from dutiful behaviour. There is thus a basic confusion in this message. A counter paradox is contained in the Chinese proverb: "Why do you wish to kill me—I have never tried to help you." (Social workers laugh perceptively when they hear this.)

ADDRESSING THE COVERT LOGIC

On our early workshops for managers we initially relied heavily on the writings of systemic family therapists, of both the strategic and structural schools (Minuchin, 1974; Selvini-Palazzoli et al., e.g. 1978; Haley, 1980; Campbell & Draper, 1985). For example, Peggy Papp (1981) describes a project to experiment with the use of paradox in treating families with symptomatic children. We progressively develop the notion of paradox, both here and in chapter six. Briefly, paradoxical interventions are those that look like the opposite of good advice but "serve to block or take to absurd lengths those problem-solving strategies that have become problems in themselves" (Simon, Stierlin, & Wynne, 1985, p. 269).

Papp's team of practitioners at the Ackerman Institute were building on the experience of other therapists, who had regretfully to admit that they had failed to help families change, although the families had claimed they wanted to change. They became aware that change was rarely a wholly rational process, and that seemingly irrational, crazy, or illogical advice was required to speak to the covert logic of the system, and to point up the absurdity or costs of the family's behaviour, before they could change. We began to feel that the results of this experience could be used in addressing role relationships between individuals, group and team dynamics, and larger organizational processes.

It has to be said that in the constantly developing practice of family therapy there is a debate raging about the meaning and efficacy of suggesting any kind of action to families. Some therapists think the family will best take care of its own plans for change, provided they have a deeper understanding of the dilemmas they are embroiled in. We think that the same question arises in relation to change in organizations, and we too have our debates. But at the moment designing interventions seems to be an important learning tool, so we continue to do it.

We have found that working in this way in an organizational context presents us with a new question: to whom is this advice addressed? We suggested earlier that a hypothesis may be offered to a client system through the manager we are talking to; or it may be addressed to the manager as part of the client system; or it may be addressed to ourselves, as those who are temporarily part of the client system too. The position is the same with respect to advice or interventions, and what follows should be read with this in mind.

STRAIGHT INTERVENTIONS

In our training work, or when facilitating peer group co-consultancy for managers, we recommend that consultants not only try to figure out a range of hypotheses about the situation presented, but also suggest interventions based on each hypothesis. We also recommend that they examine the possibilities of straight or direct interventions, before assuming that only paradox can move things along. By straight interventions we mean common-sense interventions that take no account of dynamic complexity (chapter two): providing explanations or technical know-how, advising practice, coaching new behaviour, providing training, or making detailed studies—all the usual means that organizations have at their disposal. We work on the assumption that the simpler the advice can be, the better—provided it can be followed!

Only if this straight advice does not in retrospect help the manager to improve the undesired situation should one try paradoxical methods, supposing that there must be a systemic reason why the manager has not been able to effect an obvious change. Prescribing a direct intervention will test whether the manager or system can use advice, and help the consultants see what they are up against in the organization. Straight interventions can involve advising the manager:

- to get fuller information, particularly if he or she appears to be using information selectively to substantiate his or her own prejudiced view;
- to give people information they do not usually receive;
- to bring together people who do not usually meet (e.g. in "quality circles");
- to clarify the roles of members of a working group or role-set;
- to propose or set up a process by which a management team

clarify the aims and objectives of the unit for which they are responsible.

As an example of the third option: many problems arise through an escalating exchange of memoranda, which are increasingly misunderstood, half read, or regarded with envious paranoia ("I wish I had time to spend composing this type of stuff like they do"). Straightforward advice to get the memo-writers together to talk over the situation could be a giant step forward.

The list could be extended indefinitely. Making straight interventions is like talking prose: we do it all the time. Paradoxical interventions are the poetry of consultancy practice. Direct interventions are given with the expectation that they will be followed, and will prove to be useful. It is also enhancing to the manager, as well as illuminating to the consultant, to draw out the manager's own solutions, and to support him or her in putting them into action.

Letting go of the grand plan

Harpal was the leader of a specialist social work team; she had been the leader of a hospital team previously and had picked up that role again on a temporary basis, because there was a vacancy and a review of the future of the team. Harpal asked how she could hand over this hospital team "in good order" when she ceased to be their temporary leader. The hospital was being run down, and so the future of the team was uncertain. She was unsure what to focus on in her consultation, apparently wanting to discuss her overall bewilderment and feelings of responsibility.

Questioning elicited that Harpal's sense of responsibility was directed to the hospital team as much as to the team for which she was permanently accountable. She saw the hospital team's task changing in the near future, to that of helping in-patients not to be in-patients any longer. She wished the hospital team to adopt principles and practices similar to those she had brought into her current team. Because of the uncertain future, however, when people left the hospital team they could only be replaced by temporary staff.

Our hypotheses tried to convey our sense of unreality about her wish to put a lot of work into a team that might shortly be swept away by other changes. One (linear) hypothesis put it this way:

> Harpal is putting a lot of effort into organizational change in her normal role, but also working at the hospital team level, as if there would be no changes, caught by her past work and sense of responsibility for the hospital.

This was the straight intervention given:

> Don't try to involve the hospital team in your grand plan. Be satisfied with a holding operation. Work out with the overall line manager how this new policy can be communicated to the doctor and nurse managers. Work out with the team how they want to proceed, and how to respond to pressure from these other groups.

Harpal visibly relaxed and said she had been putting great pressure on the team, ignoring the uncertainties they were already coping with. She said she could accept the limitations on the situation. The consultants did not regard this as a systemic intervention; it seemed to be logical advice, given the situation. However, clearly, it had not been logical or obvious to Harpal or her line manager.

Two months later, Harpal said she had decided to give up the temporary post of team leader. She had discussed this with her line manager and the team. She had helped the team to articulate what they wanted in the temporary team leader. She had pointed out realistically that there was no prospect for having a permanent post in the near future. She asked the team what their solution would be. The team later returned with clear proposals for their own management, and how the work required could be shared by some of the team members. Harpal thought her changed approach enabled the team to tackle their problem themselves. However, as we learned from her two months later, the proposal was scuppered by senior management, who eventually insisted on recruiting a full-time team leader. Harpal speculated that perhaps her proposal aroused anxiety about the devaluing of the management élite, by suggesting that aspects of management could be carried out by almost anyone. One could also see a paradoxical injunction in Harpal's intervention— the best way to get superiors to appoint someone is to advise the superiors that they can be done without!

PARADOXICAL INTERVENTIONS

Paradoxical interventions, as we have indicated, should only be used if the situation appears to be stuck, or if the manager has tried a number of different solutions which have only served to escalate the undesired situation.

* * *

One manager, Howard, presented his situation in a way which in effect claimed that his problem was himself: he was trying to do far too much, did not feel satisfied with the quality of his efforts, and was never able to finish anything. He added that he would be "a tough case", as he had been like that for twenty years. His line manager also thought he took on too much and has tried unsuccessfully to get him to cut down. It was clear that he was looking forward to defeating the consultants.

Questions elicited that the problem did seem to be concerned more with the way the manager behaved in his role, than with the workload itself. The team advised him not to try to change just now. They said it would be too great a shock for him and might make him feel depressed. He should be very careful, but might practise trying to give up one trivial item in his workload over the next six months.

Two months later, Howard reported that he had identified at the previous session that it was important to him to take on too much, to be the "big expert". He had asked himself: "do I want to be working this hard on my low salary?" He was now working shorter hours, felt much happier, and had negotiated agreement from his manager to do an MA on organizational change. He felt that a lot of energy had been released which was enabling him to get through his work more confidently.

* * *

This last intervention was what Peggy Papp (1981, p. 246) has called a "defiance-based" intervention. It was based on the assumption that the client had a defiant, rather than compliant, attitude to authority. Such interventions are used with individuals or groups who have a strong motivation to defeat experts who are seeking to intervene in their lives. "Compliance-based" interventions are used with those who respect and trust experts, with or without evidence of their competence.

Papp describes three major techniques used in designing and applying a systemic paradox:

- reframing (she uses the term "redefining")
- prescribing
- restraining.

The intervention (or non-intervention) given to Howard may be seen as an example of a restraining intervention. The subject is discussed further later in this chapter.

Reframing interventions

If a client group are presenting a picture in which they are victims of processes in the wider organization, one could intervene systemically by congratulating them on their willingness to sacrifice themselves for others, suggesting that the place might fall apart if they stopped. If they are irritated by this, and recoil, this may help to put them more in touch with their own powers and resourcefulness. In our own experience, however, consultants seldom provoke this kind of reaction, because in various ways they signal that this is a playful comment (see also chapter six). This is in itself a reframing, and it parallels Charles Hampden-Turner's use of humour in enabling managers to confront painful dilemmas (see chapter six).

We have already given several examples of reframing dysfunctional behaviour, construing it as a means of controlling and regulating disruptive change. Complaining about overload, manifesting stressed behaviour (sickness, lateness), not turning up to training sessions, and acting confused about seemingly clear procedures can all be redefined—in appropriate circumstances—as ways of slowing down change. A comment of this kind is itself potentially interventive, in that it can provoke new responses. Such behaviour can also be challenged (if sussed out) by asking the team: if you were *really* serious about slowing down change, how could you sabotage this management initiative even more effectively?

Reframing interventions may lead a manager into a perception of a deeper and more complex problem. For example, if she finds that she can no longer blame a subordinate for the failures of the project, she may conclude that she will have to confront *her* manager if she is to engage with the complexity of the problem, with the risk that questions might be raised about her own competence or grasp of the situation.

Prescribing interventions

A prescribing intervention is one that suggests that some kind of ritual is carried out. The covert intention of this is to block those engaged in the ritual from doing something else, or to put them in touch with each other in a fresh way.

* * *

Sarah (see also chapter three) was involved in a symmetrical power struggle with a senior worker, Robert, who did not attend staff meetings. A member of the consulting group made these suggestions to Sarah:

> Make Robert the expert—he could ask the young people what they want from the project. [It had emerged that of all staff, Robert was closest to the young people.]
>
> Recontextualize the conversation with Robert by trying to enter a neutral zone: have a rule that you and he can ask questions of each other, but nothing can be *demanded*.

The first intervention proposes that Sarah should approach Robert in a different way. The second makes more specific proposals for "recontextualized" meetings between them—that is, meetings with different ground rules. Both, if adopted, may block them from taking up their usual antagonistic pattern of relating to one another, and may create space for something different to happen between them.

Two months later, it was evident that Sarah had moved on. She said that all she could remember of the various interventions was that she should clarify Robert's role and undertake a joint task with him. It appeared that the questioning that had revealed Robert's closeness to the young people had made the manager feel better about his work and role. At a recent job evaluation, Robert had himself decided that he would be better off without management responsibility. Sarah ended by saying: "Robert has become much less significant to me, others more so; he is well down my list of worries about staff."

Beliefs and behaviour

People's beliefs, the meanings that actions and events have for them, shape the way they behave; and the way they behave shapes their beliefs. It is a recursive process. Questioning can thus be interventive when it clarifies or changes people's belief systems. This is one way of reading the situation we have just described. Robert, who was a senior worker in a project for young people with learning difficulties, was barely literate. His manager, who was trying to bring about changes in the project, tended to speak about change in abstract theoretical concepts. As Robert was closely identified with the young people, he appeared to believe that the changes would not be good for them and therefore refused to collaborate in the management aspect of his role in an effort to slow down change.

However, when Sarah, because of the fresh perspective she had gained from the consultation, changed her behaviour and acknowledged his closeness with the users as an opportunity and a strength, Robert could no longer hold on to his belief about management being dangerous. This released him to give up a management role for which he was not ready, in which he was doing his best to protect the young people, because he had begun to believe that through him their wishes were being heard.

In family therapy, prescribing interventions also include those interventions in which the client is instructed to produce the very symptom he or she is complaining of. We discuss this strategy in chapter six.

Restraining interventions

We have already given examples of restraining interventions. Earlier in this chapter, the consultants advised Howard:

> . . . not to try to change just now. They said it would be too great a shock for him and might make him feel depressed. He should be very careful, but might practise trying to give up one trivial item on his workload over the next six months.

One form of restraining intervention recommends that the manager or working group observe the problematic behaviour very carefully, but make no attempt to change it. A colleague, John Bazalgette, met with a group of staff from a secondary school, who were concerned about the increasing number of "lates" they were having to deal with each week. The group were anxious to know what should be done about it. Bazalgette advised them not to introduce any new measures for the time being, but to carry out a simple study of what was going on: Who was late? How did they travel to school? Were there more lates on a particular day of the week? Were there more latecomers from particular classes, years, or ethnic groups? In other words, could they discern any pattern in the increased lateness, which might indicate what kind of response the school could usefully make?

This intervention was both restraining and prescribing: it attempted to restrain the staff from taking additional disciplinary action, which might only make matters worse; and it suggested an activity that involved them in a different approach to the problem of lateness. It also proposed that they should ask questions and hypothesize, and so invited them to become consultants to themselves. This incident was part of an extended project to develop the school as a learning organization.

A long tradition advocates the virtues of restraining. In the sixth century BC Lao Tsu, an older contemporary of Confucius, wrote:

Who can wait quietly while the mud settles?
Who can remain still until the moment of action?
Observers of the Tao do not seek fulfilment.
Not seeking fulfilment, they are not swayed by desire for
    change.

[Gia-Fu Feng & English, 1973]

Straight interventions again

There are straight interventions that could be described as reframing, prescribing, and restraining as well. Advising a team riven by conflict to organize an "awayday" for themselves includes an element of reframing, since it implies a positive estimate of their ability to work constructively together. (It may also be a blunder, if team members attach more importance to asserting their own views than to reaching consensus.) An example of a straight prescribing intervention would be to advise a team that was destructively competitive to rotate the chair at team meetings; nothing covert is intended. Advising a team to bring in an outside consultant could sometimes be seen as a straight restraining intervention. This can be a safe and legitimate way to slow down the pace of change so that people have more time to get used to it and become committed to it.

However, no intervention can be labelled "straight" or "paradoxical" without reference to the circumstances. Advising a team that was incapable of reaching decisions to bring in an outside consultant might be a paradoxical intervention, for how could they decide whether to accept the advice or not? In our workshops, which are primarily concerned with learning, and providing consultancy is a means to that end, we sometimes ask participants to offer the problem-owner two options for action, one apparently straight and one paradoxical. This provides practice in framing interventions. In longer-term consultancy we tend to start by offering straightforward suggestions, and move into more cunning interventions if and when we become aware that we are encountering dynamic complexity (see chapter two).

We have more to learn about intervention. Family systems thinkers are at present further on than organizational consultants in designing and using interventions. So we proceed with caution to adapt some of their practices in organizations. They have, for example, been alert to the ambivalence of families towards change—how they accept the necessity of change, yet fear and resist it. Therapists working in teams have played this back to the family by means of split interventions: "The men in the therapy team believe that . . . but the women disagree, they think . . .; or: "Some of us advise this . . . and the rest of us quite the opposite". This is a way of trying to strengthen weaker elements by giving them the support of some of the team, and of handing responsibility for choice back to individuals.

* * *

We have explored the possibilities of split interventions in our own courses. In a recent course one of us (NMcC) was working in a pair with a participant to advise a manager we shall call Timothy. Timothy described a situation in which conflict between a black worker (B) and a white worker in his team had led to the white worker leaving. He was worried that this might happen again and wanted to know how he could prevent this. After a period of questioning the consultants formulated this hypothesis:

> This project has very high ideals and strong aspirations to eradicate differences between black people and white people in terms of opportunities. However, the very strength of these concerns may lead to the suppression of strong human tendencies to scapegoat difference. (There was some evidence of scapegoating, we felt, in your intention to "focus on B in the exit interviews".) We find it difficult to agree on an intervention, given this paradoxical state of affairs.

The consultants faced Timothy with this paradox by making two interventions. One wrote:

> One of us thinks you should continue to worry, because we believe in the statement made in our hypothesis, that we cannot eradicate hatred and fear of difference in our human make-up. You need to offer leadership to your whole project on this issue.

The other wrote:

> You should stop worrying about the future of the project because, as you have explained, there are no serious reasons for expecting that worker B might *cause* the next worker to leave, nor that worker B might continue to have such a divisive and hostile effect on existing colleagues. The more you worry, the more you may create doubt in the minds of others *about B.*

* * *

The most successful interventions, as Papp comments (1981, p. 246), rest on an accurate appraisal of (or inspired guess about) the relation between the symptom and the system, and the manner in which they activate one another—in other words, on the therapist's or consultant's hypothesizing flair.

We conclude this chapter with two examples of consultancy practice from our workshops, which lead up to interventions and highlight different practice issues.

LOOKING FOR LEVERAGE

Organizations, like individuals, compound their difficulties when they settle for addressing the symptoms of a problem rather than what is driving it. (We discuss the dynamics of the symptomatic solution, as analysed by Peter Senge, in more detail in chapter six.) Opting for symptomatic solutions is attractive, as they are generally quicker, cheaper, and less disruptive than more fundamental solutions (they represent a desire for change without chaos). Paula's situation, discussed in chapter three, illustrates this pattern.

Paula described her situation in this way:

> The project to which I was recently appointed has reached a mid-life point of a ten-year negotiated span. It needs to look at its source provision over the next five years. The staff are at loggerheads in two groups, managers (i.e. front-line supervisors) versus workers. The project is a residential home for young people with mental handicap and disability. A vision which is not being realized is to involve parents much more in coming into the home and physically helping staff to care for children.

One hypothesis put forward can be read as a suggestion that the conflict might have a positive function:

> This project is now in a spiralling cycle of mutual discontent between two groups of staff, because the anxiety of all the staff has been aroused by the change of project leader to one who is not a Utopian, and this has led to increased trades union activity. The wish is to avoid painful changes by blaming the situation on the incompetence of managers, who respond by reciprocal accusations of worker self-interest. This keeps the project energy focused on staff, and not on renewing their purpose, which might lead to the early demise of the project.

So the mutual accusations between managers and staff can be read as a mechanism that the total group have evolved for making the anxieties of their situation tolerable. Instead of worrying about an unpromising boss and an unknown future, they can immerse themselves in the familiar game of Us and Them. Like all symptomatic solutions (alcohol, overwork, tranquillizers), this may eventually lead to an early demise, but in the short-term it is preserving the status quo, however uncomfortably. (Interestingly, the hypothesis is ambiguous, as written: it could also mean that renewing their purpose could lead to an early demise. This may be what some people fear.)

Two suggested interventions are of particular interest. The first is this:

> Invite someone knowledgeable to give a talk to the staff on career development, and the possibilities available in the county for staff experienced in caring for multi-handicapped young people.

The intention behind this was to lessen the anxiety of staff about redundancy and lead the managers to act in a way that would be seen as responsive to staff needs. It thus addresses a basic question in framing any intervention: where in this unholy mess can we find the leverage for diverting this system onto a new course? Telling the managers and staff to stop bad-mouthing each other would be unlikely to have any leverage. This intervention is more promising, since it addresses the anxiety that is—the hypothesis proposes—driving the present self-destructive conflict.

This is the second proposed intervention:

> Create a working party of staff across the two conflicting groups, to plan a day "retreat" for re-visioning discussion for all the staff. Allow the staff group to select their own representatives.

Like the first intervention, this looks innocent enough. Yet it has a take-up-thy-bed-and-walk quality, in that it asks two groups who cannot cooperate to cooperate. So perhaps it is bound to fail. On the other hand, because the two groups will meet in a new context, and because the staff are empowered to select their own representatives, and because the retreat promises to give managers and staff ownership of the changes they most fear, perhaps it will start a new organizational story and set them on a new course. (We do not know the end of this particular story, but as we said earlier, the consultation enabled Paula to move on: at the end of the consultation she had recovered her confidence and knew what she wanted to do next.)

INCLUDING THE COMPLAINANT

Any enquiry into a situation presented by a manager or other complainant should include inviting them to "helicopter above it", and to consider the part they are themselves playing in the circular pattern of interaction. This is why the peer consultation method is potentially so useful, because it assists managers in shifting to this observer position.

* * *

Simon was a project leader in a voluntary organization. He stated his problem in this way:

> How do I close the apparent ideological gap between my management committee and the staff team I manage, so that the staff and work can be more effectively supported by the committee?

The staff believed that the committee was paternalistic, that they had a "crumbs from the table of the rich are okay for the poor" mentality. They also believed that the committee were implicitly racist and sexist: they did not understand the philosophy underlying the team's work, nor embrace actively enough the anti-racist and anti-sexist policies of the team.

Three months after the consultation, Simon commented:

> At the time, a wide variety of hypotheses were put forward. I distilled them, and adopted a hypothesis that although the gap between team and committee is not of my making, it was useful to me as a manager, since being the mediator and interpreter between committee and staff gave me a position of power and control around these issues.
>
> The gap was not as large as I may have made it. The main issue was how I was inhibiting open discussion and challenge. The feared consequences I presented, of the team challenging

the committee, for my role in the future funding of the unit, were exaggerated.

What Simon did was to arrange a team day with an outside consultant to explore race and gender issues. This was useful and constructive, and he planned to have follow-up days with the same consultant to look at specific practice and policy issues. He said the initial consultations had helped him to see that he was included in the situation he described. He now appeared to have changed his beliefs, and was operating on a new belief that perhaps he and his team colleagues were implicitly sexist and racist themselves. He was dealing with this openly, by organizing the team days. It is likely that he and his colleagues were also less preoccupied with the supposed prejudices of committee members, and therefore less inclined to adopt a morally superior position in their dealings with them.

Perhaps this was a first step—putting his own house in order. However, if it went no further than this, his programme of team days and follow-ups could also become a device for evading confrontation with the committee, perhaps in order to protect them from his team's radical views. We dislodge the stick from the reeds, and it is swept down the river until it snags in the reeds again, lower down. Systems consultation does not offer deliverance from difficulty, but only from repetition.

CHAPTER SIX

Theoretical postscript

Here comes the heavy stuff!!!

Gareth Morgan, 1993; uttered by figure in cartoon
before Morgan's theoretical appendix

I n this concluding chapter we elaborate on a number of themes
that we have touched upon in the preceding pages. We include
them here either in order to be able to examine them at greater
length, or to record ideas that have only recently come to our
attention, or to clarify how we see the relation between what is
said in this book and other bodies of theory. These are in effect five
mini-chapters or extended footnotes, related more closely to the
preceding chapters than they are to each other.

IDENTITY
AND ORGANIZATIONAL CHANGE

We have said that organizations confer an identity on their
members, and that to the extent that they become attached to these
identities, they resist organizational changes that threaten them.

Our attempts to bring about change in organizations are liable to be ineffective unless we have some understanding of what Peter Marris (1974) called "the conservative impulse" (with a small "c") by which men and women cling even to ineffective and unsatisfying structures and procedures, rather than accept and implement new ones. Marris wrote:

> The will to adapt to change has to overcome an impulse to restore the past which is equally universal. What becomes of a widow, a displaced family, a new organization or a new way of business depends on how these conflicting impulses work themselves out, within each person and his or her relationships. [p. 5]

There is a rich literature exploring this theme, drawing upon a range of concepts. Marris talks about the "context of meaning" provided by our web of social relations, which

> . . . evolves from earliest childhood, and becomes so structured and integrated that it cannot in time be radically changed without fear of psychological disintegration. [p. 17]

Writers in the Tavistock school (e.g. Menzies-Lyth, 1959; Rice, 1965) speak of the way

> . . . individuals need and use social systems as a means of maintaining their identity and protecting themselves against intolerable internal conflict. [E. J. Miller, 1976]

Individual and person

What is this identity that we defend so vigorously? Wilden (1972) and Smith and Berg (1987) assert that the concept of identity is inherently paradoxical; Wilden asks: "identical to what and to whom, for what and for whom?" (p. 260). The one who fears losing his or her identity is, from this point of view, deeply confused: for who is it that is fearing?

As a first step in clarifying the question of identity, it is useful to distinguish between two ways of thinking about human beings, corresponding to the linear and recursive views of causation. Using a distinction introduced by our former colleagues at the Grubb Institute, we will refer to these as views of a human being as an *individual*, and as a *person*.

As an *individual*, a human being is a biological entity, bounded by a skin, which is separate from other human beings and from collectivities like organizations. Every man *is* an island, entire of itself. From this point of view people join and leave organizations in the way chess pieces are placed on a board and removed when they are taken: the board and the pieces remain unchanged through these changes. This way of thinking is quite adequate for some purposes, but creates problems when it leads to an assumption that people are psychologically as well as biologically separate.

Human beings are constituted as *persons* by the network of relations and transactions of which they are a part. There is a rich literature, using various metaphors, that seeks to characterize the way the person is constituted by his or her recursive interaction with other persons (e.g. see Bateson, 1972, pp. 448ff; Zohar, 1990, pp. 107ff). It is the dominant view of the Old Testament, in which, as Abigail says to David, we are "bound together in the bundle of life". It is the view of John Donne, when he says: "And therefore never send to know for whom the bell tolls; It tolls for thee."

We might say that as persons we incorporate all our significant relations. Taking liberties with the language, we might also say that as persons we are "excorporated" in all these relations. Either way, out of our experience of these relations we crystallize a sense of a "me", which seems to have an existence of its own, which we identify with and protect from change.

However, this is not the end of the story. Various possible experiences, including the practice of spiritual disciplines or undergoing psychotherapy, may lead us to conclude that this "me", which seems so solid and important, is a construction of thought and language; to adapt Keeney's phrase, it is not illusory, but it is not real. This may become clear through learning experiences, in everyday life or in specially constructed learning events, when we find that we have not only learned to *do* something differently, but have *become* something different.

Implications

This view of personality has several implications for organizational change:

1. Managers tend to define their problems from an individual point of view. They explain their difficulties in linear terms, and their explanations do not include their own complicity in the problem, or the tacit desires that constitute their particular circumstances as a problem for them. So they generally have no difficulty with consultancy advice that treats their problem as separate from themselves. However, they are less comfortable when the consultant looks not only at what they are pointing at, but also at the person who is pointing. At this point the problem-owner is addressed as a person, and any change that takes place requires changes in the problem-owner.

2. The converse of this is also relevant. If a person is constituted by his or her network of relations, that person cannot change without others in the network changing too. At the beginning of our workshops we have sometimes adapted an exercise devised by David Campbell and his colleagues (Campbell, Draper, & Huffington, 1991a, p. 46) and asked people to consider who in their organizations or elsewhere will have to change if as a result of the course they change their own practice.

3. It also follows that those who set in hand a process of reorganization are wise if they consider how they are, to a lesser or greater degree, rejigging the *worlds*, or contexts of meaning, of those who are reorganized. Marris and others have pointed out that coming to terms with any such radical change entails grieving, just as coming to terms with the loss of a loved one entails grieving.

4. Several writers, notably Alice Miller (1983) and Robin Skynner (1989), have added another sub-plot to this story. They give reasons for supposing that individuals not only construct their identity from the associations they join, but choose organizations and types of work that provide them with a context in which they can continue to engage with conflicts in their own psyche. This may or may not be developmental for the individual and the organization. On the one hand, he (or she) may use the experiences of his work to resolve and move on from a stuckness that has persisted from childhood; on the other hand, he may be so strongly identified with this stuckness, as his way

of being himself, that he resists experiences that nudge him towards learning and change.

5. We have been impressed by the work of William Torbert and his concept of transformative leadership (Torbert, 1991; Torbert & Fisher, 1992). Torbert suggests that dysfunctional and unjust organizations can only be transformed by men and women who are capable of, and committed to, a reflexive process of learning, in which "one's very taken for granted purposes, principles, or paradigm—one's entire sense of one's life project—may be re-intuited" (Torbert & Fisher, 1992, p. 195). As this quotation may indicate, this concept of learning implies something more radical than accepting the disturbance to one's sense of identity that goes with resolving personal conflicts or living through organizational change. The catch is that, from the samples of managers Torbert has studied, it appears that very few people approach life with this kind of non-attachment to the fundamental distinctions by which they define themselves.

PARADOX

The Milan group of family therapists (Selvini-Palazzoli et al., 1978) first devised the practice of giving paradoxical instructions, as a solution to the problem of blame in families presenting a "problem" member. The problem member might be a child who refused school or a partner who made unacceptable sexual demands. As long as members of a family continue to blame one member, or each other, for their difficulties as a family, they are locked into assumptions of linear causation, which preclude acknowledgement of recursive processes within the family. Furthermore, if they accept this explanation of their difficulties, the therapists willy-nilly become part of the problem rather than part of the solution, since they endorse the blaming culture.

They evolved the practice of placing a positive connotation on the offending behaviour—refusing school, making unacceptable demands—and on the responses of other members to it. They affirmed the symptomatic behaviour as having a benign function in their life together, and cautioned the family against trying to prevent it. In this way they extricated themselves from the cycle of blaming, and bewildered the family in a therapeutic way. This kind of intervention has been called a paradoxical injunction.

We gave an example of such an injunction in chapter five. We described how a manager, Howard, blamed himself for taking on too much work. The consultants refused the invitation to take sides in Howard's internal argument, affirming his present behaviour as the best option for him at the moment.

What, then, is meant by saying that such interventions are paradoxical? There are several fascinating expositions of the concept of paradox, of which that by Watzlawick and his collaborators is the most readable (Watzlawick, Bavelas, & Jackson, 1967) (cf. Wilden, 1972; Bateson, 1972 [the "double bind"]; Selvini-Palazzoli et al., 1978; Smith & Berg, 1987). We have found that philosophical definitions of paradox are not enlightening, in the same way that definitions of a joke are not enlightening (and probably for similar reasons): the gap between the experience and the definition is too great. It may be sufficient here to say that in systemic practice we are concerned not with the paradoxes that have preoccupied philosophers, but with what have been called "existential paradoxes"; that is, with paradoxes that are lived and not merely thought about. We experience an existential paradox as "a command that can be neither obeyed or disobeyed" (Wilden, p. 104). Thus Howard—if he accepts the team's injunction—is in a fix. If he does not try to change, he implies that behaviour he has worried about for twenty years is not a problem. But if he tries to change, he rejects the advice of the consultants to whom he is looking for help.

Of course there are ways out of this fix. He can have a good laugh, which like the fear of the Lord is sometimes the beginning of wisdom. He apprehends the whole tangle he has got himself into and is released from its hold. Or he can defy his helpers, which as we said is what he actually did; and in this case he abandons his complaint and "moves on". In the circumstances of our workshop this was probably not difficult to do. The power of a paradox, positively or negatively, is proportional to the dependence of the problem-owner upon the one who gives the instruction. This is why young children are vulnerable to paradoxical communications from their parents, since to disobey their commands may be unthinkable.

The essence of a paradoxical instruction is that it can neither be obeyed nor disobeyed; or, to put it more subtly, to obey it is to disobey it, and to disobey it is to obey it. For example, we are walking along a corridor and encounter a notice that says: "No authorized persons beyond this point." If we assume that we are unauthorized persons, the notice authorizes us to proceed. But if we are authorized, surely the notice is forbidding us to proceed. So we must be unauthorized persons, who are entitled to continue beyond this point. . . . Once again, readers of this book would be unlikely to stand and dither in front of such a notice indefinitely; they would have a good laugh, or dismiss it as nonsensical. They would step outside the frame of the command. But if they were prisoners in the building, who had been told by their captors that if they disobeyed any command they would be executed, they might feel they were in an untenable position.

Apparently simple instructions like "Cheer up!" or "Go to sleep!" have the same structure; they are variations on the "Be spontaneous!" paradox, which is, once again, disobeyed if it is obeyed, and obeyed if it is disobeyed.

Watzlawick and his colleagues (1967, p. 211), following Bateson (1972, p. 206), give an example of a paradoxical maternal communication which is worth repeating, from a collection of Jewish jokes:

> Give your son Marvin two sports shirts as a present. The first time he wears one of them, look at him sadly and say in your Basic Tone of Voice: "The other one you didn't like?" [Greenburg, 1964, p. 16]

Watzlawick and colleagues say (p. 195) that the essential ingredients in a paradoxical injunction are:

1. a strong complementary relationship (parent and child, boss and subordinate, captor and prisoner [or consultant and client?]);
2. within the frame of this relationship, an injunction that can neither be obeyed nor disobeyed;
3. conditions that inhibit or prevent the one who is subject to the injunction from stepping outside the frame and so dissolving the paradox.

One steps outside the frame of a paradox by commenting on it (verbally or non-verbally), instead of trying to obey it. Howard probably did say to himself: "The so-and-so's! This is a paradoxical injunction."

The story of Marvin and his shirts illustrates the fact that a paradoxical communication is not necessarily helpful or liberating (although in this case it could be: readers may like to continue the story, describing how through this incident Marvin was finally liberated from the domination of his mother). How then can a paradoxical communication release a client or client system to move on? Watzlawick says that an intervention of this kind has to transcend ordinary common-sense advice, which assumes that people are in charge of their behaviour and can choose whether to accept the advice or not. In the case of a paradoxical intervention, choice is an illusion:

> A symptom in its essence is something unwilled and therefore autonomous. It is a piece of spontaneous behaviour, so spontaneous that it is experienced as something uncontrollable. [Watzlawick et al., p. 237]

So if the client is instructed to *produce the symptom*, this is a demand for spontaneous behaviour, which is releasing in this case whether he obeys or disobeys. If he refuses to produce the symptom, the desired change has taken place. If he produces the symptom to order, he has learned that it is under his control. So there is no escape from a benign counter-paradox, provided Watzlawick's three conditions listed above are met. Furthermore, though this is on the face of it a behaviourist approach, it can lead to changes in beliefs, including the belief that change is possible.

As we have indicated, we have experimented with interventions of this kind in our workshops and in our own work. And as we have also indicated, the working relationship between consultant and client differs in one important respect from that identified by Bateson and by Watzlawick. Consultants are generally not in a position to instruct their clients, and indeed in paid consultancy work they may be more aware that their clients are in a position to instruct *them*. There are variations on this theme: in our experience, internal consultants sometimes find that their advice is accorded the status of instruction if they are seen as close to the senior management of the organization; but they may then be more interested in using paradox to extricate themselves from that position than to capitalize on it. Certainly in our own work and in the workshops, we strive to develop a colleague relationship with our clients rather than one of dependence and hierarchical authority.

How useful, then, is the concept of paradoxical intervention in organizational consultancy? We are still exploring this question, and writing this book has required us to do so. At present this is how we see it:

1. Our aim is that whoever is in the client position should understand the recursive logic of the situations in which he or she is enmeshed, and that the client should in turn work with others enmeshed in the same problem to gain a similar understanding. Insofar as they are able to work with systemic hypotheses in this way, they are in a position to consider options for action and their probable leverage on the phenomena they regard as dysfunctional. Some of these options may turn out not to be ones that common sense would have suggested, and in this sense they could be called paradoxical. But they will not be experienced as existential paradoxes by the client.

2. It is one thing to formulate hypotheses, and another to translate them into action. We may be able to read off promising options from a hypothesis, but it is often the case that the most powerful interventions bubble up from the unconscious, and have a quirky playfulness that cannot be achieved by applying a formula. This is because the work of attending to a problem, through questioning and hypothesizing, leads to awareness of its systemic intricacy which is never wholly articulated in our hypotheses. It is therefore useful for the unconscious to have models of paradoxical interventions, like those we have discussed in this book, to chew on, so that it is better equipped to generate interventions when required.

3. It is possible for the consultant and the client to behave as though they were in a hierarchical relationship, while putting out signals that indicate to each other that they know this is only playfully intended. For example, if we had a videotape of the consultation with Howard (chapter five), we would probably notice gestures and facial expressions and tones of voice that would indicate that the team were only kidding—though in a serious way—

when they advised him not to try to change just now, and that he recognized this. In the consultation with Hugh (chapter four), the playful element is there in the text:

H: . . . I seem to be attracted to situations of extreme difficulty.
C2: Were you ever in the parachute corps?
C1: If we went on to interventions now we could congratulate you . . .
H: . . . On doing the same again. Yes.
C1: You've found the kind of work you really like!

UNCONSCIOUS PROCESSES
IN ORGANIZATIONAL LIFE

We have come to systems thinking from prior experience of work with groups and organizations using psychoanalytic concepts, based upon the premise of a dynamic unconscious. This approach explains seemingly irrational behaviour in groups and organizations as a manifestation of unconscious emotional drives, which obstruct, or sometimes reinforce, rational activity. This formative experience has a profound influence upon our work. It is also evident that many of our clients and workshop members draw upon these ideas. This section is particularly addressed to those who are familiar with the approach to organizations developed at the Tavistock Institute, and through the group relations conferences of the Tavistock and Grubb Institutes and other associations in various parts of the world (for descriptions of these conferences, see Rice, 1965; Rioch, 1979; Miller, 1989). These bring together psychoanalytic, and in particular Kleinian, concepts with the open systems model of organizations (see chapter one).

    We have been uncertain how to relate these two varieties of systems thinking and their distinctive concepts and practices. There is a linguistic complication, in that practitioners in both domains refer to their approach—rightly—as systemic. Here we shall use the terms "recursive systems thinking" and "psychodynamic systems thinking", when there is any ambiguity (cf. Reed & Armstrong, 1988). In spite of this common systemic theme, some systems thinkers dismiss the value of any reference to unconscious processes. We ourselves have headed our workshop members off psychoanalytic hypotheses, on the grounds that we were introducing them to something different. But we believe that the tendency to set up these two domains as competing accounts of the truth is ultimately destructive of understanding, whatever clarifications of position are generated by the controversy. No theory has an exclusive claim on the truth, because what is *said*, in language, can never be equated with what *is*. In T. S. Eliot's words, theories, like poetry, are no more than "raids on the inarticulate, with shabby equipment, always deteriorating". So, although we can be as sectarian as the next man or woman, our preferred selves are interested in what other raiding parties bring back from their forays.

Our position is therefore twofold. First, we believe that consultants and managers can do with as well-stocked a kit of organizational theories and interventive methods as they can find. As James Gustafson says of his own field:

> The first principle is to take the entire tradition of psychotherapy as our province for learning. The point is not to amass knowledge. No, it is rather to become familiar with what is powerful and deep in the many different guises, genres and schools which are possible in such a diverse tradition. [1986, p. 344]

Secondly, we think recursive and psychodynamic systems thinking are best regarded as two distinct languages, with some terms, like "systemic", shared by both. Keeney (1983, pp. 71f) discusses the idea that every scientific discourse is built upon one or more basic elements, or "elegant fictions", in the way classical physics was built upon the fiction of the Newtonian particle. What is the basic element in (recursive) systems thinking? He concludes by accepting the proposition that "the unit we should use as the element of behaviour is the feedback loop itself". It will be seen that our account of systems thinking in this book is developed from this starting point.

Psychodynamic systems thinking starts somewhere else. Freud regarded transference and resistance as the two definitive concepts of psychoanalysis. Underlying both of these is the fundamental premise of the dynamic unconscious itself. The group relations approach to organizations (e.g. Miller & Rice, 1967, pp. 3–24) combines this with the quite distinct premise of the open system.

These two varieties of systems thinking make little use of each other's fundamental terms. Recursive systems writers (with the exception of Bateson) seldom refer to unconscious processes. Psychodynamic systems writers say little about the recursive communication processes that (we might say) generate the phenomena they describe—though once again there are exceptions (e.g. Laing, 1961, 1970; Levenson, 1983). Prudent consultants stick within one discourse once they are using it, since the discourses are not ultimately assimilable by one another. For example, the components of Senge archetypes are behaviours that influence other behaviours: we have found that the archetypes fall apart if one includes supposed mental states as components.

We should, however, refer to the work of Gregory Bateson, who has perhaps been the greatest single influence on the development of recursive systems thinking. He regarded himself as extending the elucidation of mental processes that Freud began, rather than setting up a competing theory:

> Freudian psychology expanded the concept of mind inwards to include the whole communication system within the body—the autonomic, the habitual, and the vast range of unconscious process. What I am saying expands mind outwards. And both of these changes reduce the scope of the conscious self. [1972, p. 461]

Bateson's view of mental processes is therefore more comprehensive than that which locates them, in our muddled way, inside people's heads. The feedback loops and more complex patterns mapped out in this book are, in his terms, mental processes. We alluded to one of the consequences of this view in another quotation by Bateson, in our Introduction. Conscious thought is habitually unwise and, without access to unconscious recursive processes, eventually destructive. It understands the world in terms of linear causation, and hence sees only incomplete arcs of circles, without knowing that they are arcs. Bateson redefines wisdom as recognition of circuitry (i.e. circularity). This is why we say that recursive systems thinking is a wise approach to organizational affairs. But his statement is also, in a paradoxical way, a warning. For our hypotheses are necessarily conscious, and therefore necessarily lacking: they leave out what is still unconscious (cf. Boxer and Palmer, 1993). The raid on the inarticulate may bring back useful booty; but the inarticulate is still there, and there is more where it came from.

This is an implicit critique of much consultancy, group work, and organizational development, within both domains of systems thinking. Consultants talk about taking a "meta" position, as though there were a position from which they could speak which was not local and one-eyed. They may speak from a position that is different from that of the client, but what they say is necessarily shaped by their own conscious and unconscious preconceptions. Others make psychoanalytic interpretations without questioning their own position, as though everything that can be usefully and illuminatingly said can be said from a psychoanalytic viewpoint. We forget that, after all our hard intellectual and emotional work, our interpretations, hypotheses, and interventions come to us out of the blue, out of the void, out of nowhere. If they do not turn up, there is nothing we can do about it, except have a cup of coffee or go for a walk. Consequently, when they do turn up, we take big risks, with ourselves and with our client organizations, if we do not scrutinize them carefully to try to see how they have been shaped by unconscious processes—by our own desires, and by the desires immanent in the larger circuits of which we are a part:

> Since a consultancy project is an episode in the life of the consultant, as well as in the lives of others who make up the client system, becoming aware of the Real problem means becoming aware of a question about what *we* are up to, as well as what other people are up to—the question of our own desire. [Boxer & Palmer, 1993]

SYSTEMS ARCHETYPES

A few years ago our workshops on systems thinking, and our own practice, were limited by the fact that we had no settled idea of what a well-formed systemic hypothesis might look like. Whilst every organizational problem is in its specifics unique, we suspected that there must be themes, as there are in family therapy. This was evident from the fact that, when someone describes an organizational problem, other people's questions and comments show that they believe they recognize what is going on, even though they have heard nothing about this specific situation previously.

We were therefore immediately interested when a member of an earlier workshop, John Nurse, drew our attention to the work of Peter Senge. In *The Fifth Discipline* (1990), Senge expounds what he regards as the five core disciplines that are required in creating a learning organization. The fifth discipline, and the cornerstone of the learning organization, is systems thinking, and in particular an understanding of positive and negative feedback. Senge shows how positive and negative feedback loops can be used as building blocks to assemble the patterns of interaction that he suggests underlie many organizational and social problems. He thus provides us with a set of about a dozen templates, which he calls systems archetypes, for formulating hypotheses. We used one of these templates, the "Limits to Growth" archetype, in chapter four. Senge explains the value of the archetypes in this way:

> Mastering the systems archetypes starts an organization on the path of putting the systems perspective into practice. It is not enough . . . to appreciate basic systems principles. It is not even enough to see a particular structure underlying a particular problem (perhaps with the help of a consultant). *This can lead to solving a problem, but will not change the thinking that produced the problem in the first place.* . . . Only when managers start thinking in terms of the systems archetypes, does systems thinking become an active daily agent, continually revealing how we create our reality. [p. 95]

We have not yet made use of all the archetypes in our own work, and we shall not discuss them all here. We suggest that the reader follows us in practising using two or three of the simpler archetypes, and then progressively adds to his or her repertoire if this approach to hypothesizing seems useful. This will entail buying or borrowing Senge's book! We also recommend getting the hang of the archetypes by using them to generate hypotheses about situations in the newspapers or in history or literature. How, for example, would you represent the attempt to reduce traffic congestion by building more roads? Or the way the "glass ceiling" operates to prevent women getting top jobs? Or the ineffectiveness

SHIFTING THE BURDEN

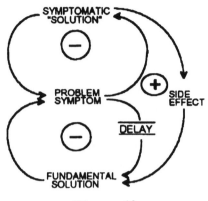

Diagram 10

of legal sanctions in limiting alcohol or drug abuse in a society (cf. chapter two)?

We have encountered many situations that correspond to a pattern Senge calls "Shifting the Burden"; it might also have been called "The Symptomatic Solution". This maps out many familiar situations in which a short-term solution is used to relieve a pressing problem, and is for a while successful. However, because the underlying source of the problem has not been addressed, sooner or later it reappears. The short-term or symptomatic solution is again applied, but with more short-lived results, so that it has to be used again more and more frequently. The use of the symptomatic solution is not only increasingly disappointing and perhaps expensive; it also undermines the capability of those concerned to find a fundamental solution. The archetype may be represented as in Diagram 10.

One of us (BP) found this archetype illuminating in trying to understand the behaviour of the members of a social work team, who organized an "awayday" to talk about their overwork and low morale. One way of reading their situation was to say that their problem was the increasing number of demanding child-protection cases for which they were responsible. They solved this problem by working longer hours. This staved off imagined disasters, but was of limited effectiveness: the rate of referrals went on increasing, and the social workers became more and more exhausted. Furthermore, their tiredness and suppressed anger reduced their capacity to face what might be entailed in finding a fundamental solution. They saw this as being willing to say "No" to referrals that were beyond their reasonable capacity to deal with; but this would require sanction from their divisional manager, whom they did not expect to support any such proposal. (They were rescued—if that is the right word—by a major reorganization, before a crisis point was reached.)

Senge implies that there are fundamental solutions as well as symptomatic solutions to all problems. He glosses over the possibility that there may be no solution to some undesired situations. More seriously, he treats problems and solutions as though they were real, rather than being constructed by persons out of circumstances and their own desires (cf. chapter two).

We can illustrate this with a London example—the colony of homeless people currently living in tents and boxes in a central city square, Lincoln's Inn Fields. This causes concern and fear to local residents and workers and to passers-by. There have been complaints that the presence of the colony lowers the tone of this up-market square, is unhygienic, unhealthy for the homeless, creates beggars, and has led to muggings and vandalism. Compassionate groups have set up soup runs—currently forty-one per week. A central government "initiative for rough sleepers" has ploughed a large sum of money into the development of hostel beds in the capital. This has made little impact on the numbers of sleepers in Lincoln's Inn Fields.

Both the provision of food and blankets by voluntary groups, and the provision of hostel accommodation by the government, may have to be seen as symptomatic solutions—they make the givers feel better. Housing aid workers would say the problem is much more complex than a short-term lack of a roofed bed space and reflects a strategic failure to build houses and provide cheap renting accommodation; and that this is coupled with the economic recession, the severity of which is a consequence of the present government policies. They would also point out that the closure of large hospitals for the mentally ill and mentally handicapped has not been successful for a percentage of ex-patients, who find they cannot live with relatives or manage on their own. Thus the search for a solution brings into view widening interlocking circuits of causation, rather than a closed system within which what would count as a fundamental solution can be defined.

We have tried to convey something of the elegance and usefulness of the system archetypes, and also our reasons for adding a health warning. The very clarity of the archetypes is a snare, and one of which Senge himself seems not to be aware. Using them, it is easy to confuse the map with the territory, and to slip into thinking that we are constructing the true description of what is going on; whereas, as we have said several times, no hypothesis can be more than a "take" on what is going on, from a particular perspective. The archetypes identify problem situations, gaps, delays, and solutions as though they had an existence of their own. It is wise, therefore, to construct alternative descriptions, to note carefully information that does not fit our preferred hypothesis, and to be ready to revise our hypotheses continually as we make interventions and receive feedback.

MAPPING DILEMMAS

Many organizational impasses can be interpreted as the consequence of trying to implement aims and values that are integral to the character or identity of the organization, and yet mutually conflicting, at least in the way they are pursued. We were introduced to this way of looking at stuckness in terms of *dilemmas* through the work of Charles Hampden-Turner (1987, 1989, 1990; see also his Foreword). Hampden-Turner takes further the analysis of problems initiated by Watzlawick (see chapter two): the form of hypothesis to which this gives rise is a way of reframing a presenting problem. One of Hampden-Turner's beliefs is that because organizational dilemmas arouse strong feelings, they are best addressed through humour, and this belief informs his writing, which is liberally illustrated with cartoons.

A dilemma is a di-lemma. A "lemma" is a premise or proposition in logic. Hampden-Turner proposes that organizational problems can frequently be represented as attempts to act on incompatible premises. The manager or practitioner must find ways of avoiding being impaled on the horns of this di-lemma. He or she must endeavour to navigate between them, like Odysseus sailing between the rock Scylla and the whirlpool Charybdis.

So, for example, a manager evaluating subordinates may experience himself or herself as torn between evaluating their performance disinterestedly and maintaining a collaborative and trusting relationship with them (Hampden-Turner, 1990, p. 124ff) . The dilemma may be stated in the form of a question:

> Given the obvious desirability of paying employees according to the value of their performance to the company, is it possible to achieve this while maintaining authentic communications and mutually sustaining relationships?

Hampden-Turner sketches the hazards between which the supervisor steers, or fails to steer, in this way:

> The "rock" of too eager imposition of the organization's standards via increments of reward is called the *Cold Appraisal*. The "whirlpool" of infinite concern for the feelings of employees is called *Sensitive and Safe*. This occurs when a supervisor anxious at all costs to remain on friendly terms with a poorly performing employee, is tactful about incompetence. [p. 126]

He maps out the possible options diagrammatically. The cunning of these diagrams is that they do not represent the two "lemmas" as in opposition to each other, but at right angles, as depicted in Diagram 11. This diagram immediately suggests that there may be many ways of behaving in relation to the two basic premises of "evaluation and pay according to performance" and "open relationships and communications". So far only two have been named: "sensitive and safe", at position 10:0, and "the cold appraisal", at position 0:10. What would it mean to conform in some degree to both premises, at position 3:3, say, or 5:5, or 8:8? And what would it be like to operate in the 10:10 position, conforming fully to both premises? Is such a position imaginable?

In our workshops we have found this approach to hypothesizing powerful and releasing. For example, Mark was responsible for making changes in the way an education department provided social work services to children from ethnic minorities. He foresaw

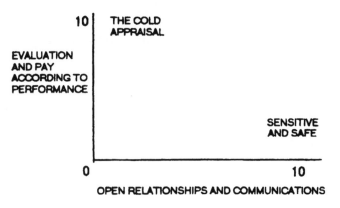

Diagram 11

destructive conflict between the black staff and the white staff who would implement this scheme. His question was:

How can I help these two sets of staff to cope with these changes without hurting one another?

After exploring the situation, including Mark's own ideals and anxieties, in some depth, one of us mapped out his dilemma as in Diagram 12. The 10:10 position was identified by Mark and is incorporated in the horizontal and vertical axes. It was a state of affairs in which collaboration based on an awareness of common humanity was enriched by awareness of, and respect for, ethnic and other differences. The other positions are self-explanatory.

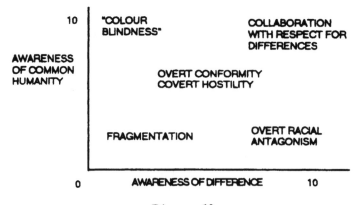

Diagram 12

Organizational life is characterized by recurring dilemmas: centralization/decentralization; generic work/specialist work; speed of service delivery/minimizing errors. Hampden-Turner suggests (1989) that organizations that fail to identify and synergize the dilemmas on which they are impaled lurch from one horn to the other. So, for example, they decentralize (on the premise that people work more creatively when they have control over their own affairs, and decisions are made close to the coal-face). Then they become concerned that the organization has no coherent corporate strategy, and re-centralize again. Mapping dilemmas of this kind is a way of positioning oneself outside all the activity and seeing it whole. In Cronen and Pearce's terms (see chapter three), one is proposing a meaning for the activity as an organizational story, with the possibility of discovering a strategy for effective intervention.

Hampden-Turner suggests (1990, pp. 117ff) a series of techniques for working towards wise interventions:

1. *Elicit* and describe the dilemmas, humorously, to enable people to distance themselves from premises to which they are strongly committed.

2. *Map* each dilemma and name the possible positions (as we have done above).

3. *Process* each dilemma by turning nouns into verbs: "criticizing", not "criticism". This softens the dilemma, turning hard positions into softer activities.

4. See what the possibilities are when one horn is made the *context* of the other: for example, is it possible to build a culture of open communications and trust, so that when the time for performance appraisal comes around, the necessary hard-nosedness will be acceptable because it is in a context of mutual confidence?

5. Explore the scope for *sequencing* initiatives: that is, moving first horizontally, then vertically, towards the 10:10 position. In other words, consider that it may not be necessary to act upon both premises simultaneously. For example, is it possible for local managers to move periodically between the centre and the periphery, so that they build up both local and corporate perspectives on the work of the organization?

6. *Synergize* dilemmas. This is a way of testing how effectively the previous steps have been carried out. The question is whether we have created virtuous rather than vicious circles, or discovered how "the whole system has an intelligence which its parts lack" (1990, p. 143). For example, one might ask employees: "Do you feel that the criticisms you get in your appraisal interviews contribute to improving your relationship with your supervisor?"

Hampden-Turner also implies that one should encourage *modesty of expectation*. We should not expect to live in the 10:10 position. "You are never at this point; you are always getting there" (1989). Sometimes it will be achieved, but often we will be living with compromises or oscillating between different positions. But we will be less likely to make this difficulty into a problem, because we have a map of the terrain we are in.

Underlying the theory of dilemmas is an important insight about organizations. To get things done, we have to imagine organizations as coherent systems with shared aims, objectives, and organizational assumptions. But from time to time we run up against problems—like those we have been describing—that can only be understood if we let go of our dream of a coherent organization. Instead, we adopt the metaphor of the dilemma: that organizations are constructed out of an array of premises, held by the same and different people, and these premises are not necessarily mutually compatible. If they are accorded the force of unquestionable principles, then the scene is set for oscillation between opposing configurations, and for debilitating conflict which rumbles on forever. In such circumstances only an approach to hypothesizing that identifies the conflicting premises and puts them all on one map may have a chance of providing leverage.

How we introduce course participants to systems practice

In our courses on systems thinking and practice, we have worked with third- and fourth-tier managers, department and regional heads, team leaders and section heads, and also with staff in training and development, administration, fund-raising, and information. To date these managers have been drawn from health and welfare settings, voluntary child care organizations and agencies serving families, and the probation service. Courses have comprised between ten and fifteen participants, with two tutors. The most recent have offered the opportunity for those who have taken part in previous courses to work together as a separate "returners" group for part of the time.

Often there have been participants from different levels in the same organization. We have arranged for them to work in different groups when possible, but this has seemed to matter little to them, perhaps because the climate of the course is one of objectivity, neutrality, and recognition of systemic processes. Similarly, our relatedness to the participants has generally been easy, friendly, and open. We avoid stimulating projections onto ourselves as authority figures, which can often get in the way of learning. This is also a characteristic of the method itself—adopting what is called a "one-down" position in the face of resistance to change.

THE CONSULTATION EXERCISE

The core activity of our course is the consultation exercise. We repeat this several times, using the course participants' own selected situations to work on. We back this up with detailed explanations of the theory behind the different stages of the consultation exercise, and with sessions on systems theory or related topics. Other shorter exercises may be introduced, to enable participants to take on board this paradoxical way of thinking, to make a point to a particular group, or as icebreakers to introduce people to one another at the beginning of a course.

When we accept managers onto our courses, we invite them to select a work situation that is causing them perplexity, difficulty, or a feeling of stuckness. We assure them that this does not have to be framed in a systemic way; they may tell their story in their own words to other course participants, whom we shall guide in a particular way to explore the situation and hopefully suggest some useful options for action. One of our first actions on the course is to work out some ground rules about safeguarding confidentiality between participants, some of whom, as we have said, may come from the same organization, and all of whom could probably network with each other's colleagues. Participants appear to trust each other's professional ethics in this regard, although some tend to offer safer situations than others, who take more of a risk with their reputation for competence.

We get people started on the consultation exercise with minimal theoretical introduction. This is a demonstration of our confidence in the potency of the exercise itself as a discipline and in their competence and motivation to make use of it. To demonstrate the stages of work to everyone in the same way, we start off working as a total course group. The procedure, which is not rigid and is still evolving, is at present as follows.

1. *Presentation and clarification:* One participant is asked to present his or her selected work situation while the others act as consultants. One of the tutors (or a participant) asks clarifying questions, to draw out necessary detail in as neutral a way as possible, so that the context and problematic issues can be grasped sufficiently for the participants to begin to have a view about them. This does not usually take more than ten or fifteen minutes, and we encourage the presenter to stick to "facts" in the first instance. The aim is to find out how long the situation has been going on and who is involved, to get a detailed description of the behaviour or attitudes that cause concern to the presenter, and to take the first steps to explore what may be a patterning of behaviour around the problem. This initial exploration should include finding out what steps they have already taken, if any, to remedy the situation described. This may indicate that attempted solutions have become part of the escalation of the problem. This initial clarification concludes when we find we are beginning to distinguish recurring patterns of interaction, which suggest circular rather than linear processes of cause and effect. This indicates that we are ready to go on to the next stage.

2. *Re-telling:* At this point we suggest that pairs of participants discuss together what they have made of the situation so far, and to write a brief "re-telling" that summarizes the picture they have built up (see also chapter four). This may be no more than an attempt to reflect back what they have heard, or it may include an element of interpretation. They then read their re-tellings to the presenter, who has the opportunity to comment.

3. *Questioning:* The same pairs are then asked to frame two or three questions they would like to put to the presenter to test out their assessment or hunch about what is going on. We limit the number of questions in order to help them focus on key connections, and to learn to link exploration to incipient hypotheses. The presenter answers the questions as best he or she can, but we discourage free discussion at this point.

4. *Hypothesizing:* We then suggest to the participants that, having heard all the questions put by course members and tutors and the answers given by the presenter, they have probably devel-

oped their views about the situation, and how the presenter is involved in it. We ask them to take fifteen minutes or so to frame a hypothesis about the problem and what is causing it. We ask them to write this on a card, as succinctly as possible, and later to share it with the presenter. It is of course initially very difficult to do this, and quite alarming to have to commit oneself on paper to a specific explanation of what one has heard. Under this pressure, participants tend to fall back upon linear, cause-and-effect explanations, fixing blame on the presenter or someone the presenter has mentioned. As the course continues, with the tutors attempting to model more systemic hypotheses, these explanations become more circular and neutral in form and propose how various individuals and groups, some not directly involved in the situation, contribute to perpetuating it. The presenter has an opportunity to respond to these hypotheses, and he or she often come up with new information at this point. We frequently ask the presenter to work out and share his or her own hypothesis.

5. *Interventions:* Finally, on the strength of the hypotheses they have worked out or heard from others, the pairs of participants are invited to recommend specific proposals to the presenter, about what he or she could do (or ignore) to change the sequence of events that is causing concern. The pairs are asked to write these on another card, which is handed to the presenter with an explanation if asked for. We ask for the presenter's feedback as to whether he or she could do the actions proposed, how they would feel about it, and what possible outcomes there might be. Presenters take these cards away with them as a tangible result from the course, and in follow-up sessions they have often referred to them and the use they decided to make of them (or not).

This whole process, of demonstrating the method and feeding in teaching about hypotheses, and about categories of questions that are useful, can take two or three hours. The process is repeated more speedily by working in smaller groups, with the tutors choosing to join a group, to move around, or just to be available for consultation on aspects of the process, whatever seems most useful at the time.

INTRODUCTORY SESSIONS

There has always been a difficulty about how to start off the course. In earlier years we spent a lot of time—too much, we feared—in encouraging participants to share their working contexts with each other in interesting and visual ways—for example, by making plasticine models, or by drawing. We decided to drop this, partly because it led to information overload, and partly because it took almost a day to prepare and share the information. However, we still have regrets about this, as managers often gained considerable insight about their teams from engaging in this process.

In more recent courses we have used less elaborate exercises, which both enable the participants to say something about themselves, and also introduce them to systems thinking. We give two examples later. The first session of the course also includes a first look at some systems concepts.

THEORY SESSIONS

We have progressively developed participative ways of introducing course members to relevant theories. When we started there was little published literature on systems thinking, or certainly not in the UK, that was relevant to organizations and management. We drew heavily and somewhat uneasily on the large body of systemic thinking, research, and practice used in therapeutic work with families. Many of our initial course participants were involved directly in social work practice, and had some training in family therapy. We thus had at least a core of participants who spoke the same language. However, one or two of our course members were overtly critical of our theoretical focus on families, and quite rightly challenged our assumption that what held good for families as systems could also apply to teams and organizations. We were usually at pains to have course members work at what they saw were the differences and similarities between families and teams. Gradually, over the last few years, we have turned to the developing literature relevant to behaviour in organizations.

In some theory sessions we might ask members to read a seminal chapter on some aspect of the consulting process. It could be on problem definition or common organizational dilemmas. We might then ask them to discuss the reading in pairs, share their individual interpretations of its meaning and relevance to their work, and come together in a group to share what seemed most striking to those present.

We have also invited members to explore together certain key concepts such as power—the meaning and exercise of it. We would start by drawing on their own experience of power, collecting their comments on a flip chart. Then we would discuss the propositions of various systems thinkers relevant to this, either confirming or adding to the ideas of the course members. We would provide participants with a short further-reading list and a summarizing handout. However, the vitality and interest of the course seems to be located for the members in the consulting exercises. They have not wished to plunge too deeply into the work of systems theorists, some of which seems complicated and obscure to people with a non-scientific background.

OTHER LEARNING METHODS

In view of this, we look for ways of introducing systems theory more playfully. For example, in presenting Cronen and Pearce's theory of the Coordinated Management of Meaning (see chapter three), we began on one occasion by drawing and explaining to the participants the diagram the authors use, showing how contexts of a "speech act" fit into one another like Chinese boxes. We then illustrated the use of the diagram with a quote from a Barbara Pym novel, showing how we began to construct contexts at various levels, in order to make sense even of one remark. Finally we played a short game of consequences with them, and in pairs invented a context that made sense of the resulting crazy stories.

We try not to repeat exercises simply because they have gone well; rather, we try to remain as tutors on an edge of change and uncertainty similar to that on which the participants must sometimes feel themselves. We try to create learning experiences that will fit the situation in the here and now. For example, at the beginning of a course, to draw attention to the feedback loops that link people in organizations, we might ask course members to interview each other in pairs, and to find out who would lose and who would gain in that member's context if the course was successful in helping him or her to learn. Another time we might ask course members to suggest three different ways in which they could sabotage the work of the course. This makes the assumption that making one's potential deviance public acts as a block to enacting it!

More recently, use of the Senge (1990) systems archetypes has proved a productive source of learning about circularity, and about common and inevitable organizational tangles. Because they are presented visually, they provide a clarity of explanation, even to novices, which had previously been missing in our courses. In one session, the participants were asked to look over a series of diagrams depicting these archetypes. They then selected a situation in their work, in society, or in international relations and matched it with an archetype that seemed to explain what was going on. We were impressed how quickly the participants grasped the sense of these organizational forces, and we feel certain that it was because a visual medium was used rather than a lecture or discursive method of teaching.

The value of playfulness

We have used role-play to introduce the theme of organizational dilemmas (see chapter six). We might ask some members to role-play a scene in which members of the Royal Family advise one another about how to remain in the daily consciousness of the nation, without stimulating prurient curiosity and publicity. We might then move on to an organizational theme, asking a manager to enlist other participants in role-playing a vexed situation in his own team. They would then be given suggestions about what was going on in the team, and how they handled the situation—defusing it wisely or escalating it. We would suggest methods of observation that focused on process and pattern rather than content—the choreography rather than the steps.

This kind of exercise broaches the subject of the typical games people play in organizations, which in turn reflect the painful dilemmas that arise between focusing on task or on process, on results or on the people employed to obtain them.

The value of creating exercises of this kind has been underlined by David Campbell and his colleagues, who provide instructions for a series of exercises (1991a, pp. 43ff). We adapted one of these for one of our courses. The odd thing was that the participants misheard or disobeyed the instruction; and their reactions to the exercise became such a fulcrum for learning about systems that they could hardly bear to end the subsequent discussion. The purpose of the exercise was to show how we accommodate ourselves to work systems. The instruction was:

> Form into two circles of eight. Each person think about what role they would like to play if this were to be a new work system. Then say in sequence: "If the previous person were to behave in a role in that way, then I would want to behave in such and such a way."

This sequence was to continue for three or four circuits of the group. One group conformed to the instruction. The other did not: one or two members refused to speak. The groups were thus superficially dissimilar in behaviour, and yet similar, as it turned out, in their covert wishes to resist the instructions, which were suppressed by the first group and by the law-abiding members of the second.

Exercises of this kind have the aim of engaging participants, experientially and playfully, in a group experience. We believe that playfulness is an important and liberating mode of learning. Role playing and group exercises are forms of serious play. (We have taken up this term from Colin Evans. If we suppose that our lives include periods of work and periods of play, each of which can be either trivial or serious, then there are four possibilities: trivial work, serious work, trivial play, and serious play: see Evans & Palmer, 1989.)

TESTING WHAT HAS BEEN LEARNED

Initially, we ran the course for five or six days, in two or three parts. After each module there was a three-month gap. In the second module, participants were asked to retrace the steps of the situation they had presented in the first part, and to recount what they had since initiated or had changed their minds about. They told us how the situation was now. This was useful feedback to the tutors, both for evaluating the method and for the writing of this book. The situation was rarely, if ever, quite the same. We have to admit that sometimes it was worse: the problem behaviour had escalated. However, we later learned that this had brought a resolution. Other times a "problem" person had disappeared as a focus, and something else appeared more urgent; when explored, it was usually possible to view the disappearance from focus as a reframing that put the problematic relations in a new perspective.

But then, as the economic recession made it difficult for health and welfare staff to obtain funding for a five- or six-day residential course, we decided in 1993 to pilot a three-day module with separate groups for "returners" and "beginners" for the consultation exercise. One of us worked with each group. This worked well: our first such course was over-subscribed, and several beginners made a bid to return to the next course, scheduled for six months later. We have decided to stick with this pattern for the time being, although for the tutors and possibly the participants it has disadvantages: tutors and participants are prevented from learning together (and differently) from the same material; the beginners no longer have the more experienced participants as models; and we can less readily find out what has happened as a result of the interventions offered.

However, for the participants it has the added value that in the concluding session we feel able to let go of a monopoly on the tutor role. The returners are invited to be consultants to the beginners, with access to advice from the tutors if they request it. This has worked well for both groups, and it offers the returners a real opportunity for testing what they have learned.

Before embarking on this concluding exercise the consultants (returners) and consultees (beginners) meet separately, and list what they consider to be the skills of a good consultant or client. The consultants' list has included:

- Avoid taking a one-up position. Avoid dominating or arguing with the client.
- Listen to clients attentively and actively. Listen to what is not said.
- Ask open questions, and funnel down to specifics.
- Question assumptions, including one's own
- Avoid information overload; use summarizing, re-telling.

- Be flexibly systematic, explain the process, establish and work to a contract, convey orderliness.
- Signal paradox; use humour, playfulness.
- Avoid having a mental map that excludes relevant influences and contexts.
- Pay attention to role boundaries and the limit or extent of authority.
- Do not immediately focus on the organization's agenda or your own agenda for this contact: start where the client is.
- Find out the client's feelings about the issues.

After the exercise, we return to these lists. In a fishbowl configuration, the consultants discuss how they have got on, while the consultees listen. Then the consultees discuss how they have got on, while the consultants listen. This procedure is valuable in giving all the participants an opportunity to identify skills that have been used (or not used) but not identified in the preceding two days of the course. From an evaluation point of view, it also gives the tutors a good idea of how effective the consultations have been.

ENDING

We tend to use both linear and circular methods of evaluation in the closing session of the course. Participants may be asked to give succinct feedback under four headings: appreciations, regrets, illuminations, and requests for the future. This method has been criticized as a rather linear way of going about it, but we feel it gives us differentiated information from each member and allows them to express disappointments as well as achievements and learning. We have also asked participants to suggest three ways in which they could assist their organizations in preventing them from using what they had learned on the workshop, in the hope that the participants would thus be stimulated defiantly to ensure that they did not give their teams and colleagues any such opportunities.

For information about these workshops, contact Nano McCaughan, The Children's Society, Edward Rudolf House, Margery Street, London WC1X 0JL (071-837 4299); or Barry Palmer, 42 Tufnell Park Road, London N7 0DT (071-263 3209)

REFERENCES

Argyris, C., & Schon, D. A. (1978). *Organizational Learning: A Theory of Action Perspective*. Reading, MA: Addison-Wesley.

Bateson, G. (1972). *Steps to an Ecology of Mind*. New York: Ballantine.

Bateson, G. (1979). *Mind and Nature*. London: Wildwood.

Bazalgette, J., & French, R. B. (1993). *From "Learning Organization" to Teaching-Learning Organization*. London: The Grubb Institute.

Berne, E. (1966). *Games People Play*. London: Deutsch.

Bion, W. R. (1961). *Experiences in Groups*. London: Tavistock.

Bleich, D. (1978). *Subjective Criticism*. Baltimore, MD: Johns Hopkins University Press.

Boxer, P., & Palmer, B. W. M. (1993). *Passing Beyond the Problem as Presented: What Do We Do Next?* (Seminar notes, May 1993, for publication.)

Brewer's Dictionary of Phrase and Fable (1981). London: Cassell.

Bruggen, P., & O'Brian, C. (1987). *Helping Families: Systems, Residential and Agency Responsibility*. London: Faber.

Campbell, D., & Draper, R. (1985). *Applications of the Milan Approach to Family Therapy*. London: Grune & Stratton.

Campbell, D., Draper, R., & Huffington, C. (1991a). *Teaching Systemic Thinking*. London: Karnac Books.

127

Campbell, D., Draper, R., & Huffington, C. (1991b). *A Systemic Approach to Consultation*. London: Karnac Books.

Cecchin, G. (1987). Hypothesizing, circularity and neutrality revisited: an invitation to curiosity. *Family Process, 26*: 405–413.

Checkland, P. (1981). *Systems Thinking, Systems Practice*. Chichester/ New York: Wiley.

Cooper, L. W., & Gustafson, J. P. (1992). *From Old to New Stories in Organizations*. Unpublished.

Cronen, V., & Pearce, W. B. (1980). *Communication, Action and Meaning: The Creation of Social Realities*. New York: Praeger.

Cross, A. (1990). *A Trap for Fools*. London: Virago.

Evans, C., & Palmer, B. W. M. (1989). Inter-group encounters of a different kind: the experiential research model. *Studies in Higher Education, 14* (3): 297–308.

Garlick, H. (1990). Leaning on the oldest profession. *The Guardian*, 10 October.

Garratt, B. (1990). *Creating a Learning Organization*. Englewood Cliffs, NJ: Prentice-Hall.

Gia-Fu Feng, & English, J. (trans.) (1973). *Tao Te Ching*, by Lao Tsu. London: Wildwood.

Greenburg, D. (1964). *How to Be a Jewish Mother*. Los Angeles, CA: Price/Stern/Sloan.

Gustafson, J. P. (1986). *The Complex Secret of Brief Psychotherapy*. New York/London: Wiley.

Gustafson, J. P. (1992). *Self-Delight in a Harsh World*. New York/London: Norton.

Haley, J. (1980). *Leaving Home*. New York: McGraw-Hill.

Hampden-Turner, C. (1987). *AIDS—The Next Twenty-Five Years: Mobilising Society's Resources*. London: The Grubb Institute.

Hampden-Turner, C. (1989). *Corporate Culture and the Management of Dilemma*. London: London Business School.

Hampden-Turner, C. (1990). *Charting the Corporate Mind: From Dilemma to Strategy*. Oxford: Blackwell.

Hare, D. (1993). *Asking Around*. London: Faber.

Hein, P. (1969). *Grooks*. London: Hodder.

James, W. (1943). *Essays in Pragmatism*. New York: Haffner.

Keeney, B. P. (1983). *Aesthetics of Change*. New York: Guilford.

Laing, R. D. (1961). *The Self and Others*. London: Tavistock.

Laing, R. D. (1970). *Knots*. London: Tavistock.

Levenson, E. A. (1983). *The Ambiguity of Change*. New York: Basic Books.

Marris, P. (1974). *Loss and Change.* London: Routledge (revised edition, 1986).

Maturana, H. R., & Varela, F. J. (1987). *The Tree of Knowledge.* Boston/London: Shambala.

Menzies-Lyth, I. (1959). The functioning of social systems as a defence against anxiety. Reprinted in *Containing Anxiety in Institutions.* London: Free Associations, 1988.

Miller, A. (1983). *The Drama of the Gifted Child.* London: Faber.

Miller, E. J. (Ed.) (1976). *Task and Organization.* London/New York: Wiley.

Miller, E. J. (1989). *The "Leicester Model": Experiential Study of Group and Organizational Processes.* London: Tavistock.

Miller, E. J., & Rice, A. K. (1967). *Systems of Organization.* London: Tavistock.

Minuchin, S. (1974). *Families and Family Therapy.* London: Tavistock.

Morgan, G. (1986). *Images of Organization.* Beverly Hills/London: Sage.

Morgan, G. (1993). *Imaginization.* Newbury Park/London: Sage.

Palmer B. W. M., & Reed B. D. (in preparation). *An Introduction to Organizational Behaviour.* London: The Grubb Institute. (Original edition 1972.)

Palmer, B. W. M., & McCaughan, N. M. (1988). All in a day's work. *Community Care* (2 June): 21ff.

Papp, P. (1981). Paradoxes. In S. Minuchin & H. C. Fishman (Eds.), *Family Therapy Techniques.* Cambridge, MA: Harvard University Press.

Pedler, M., Burgoyne, J., & Boydell, T. (1991). *The Learning Company.* London/New York: McGraw-Hill.

Reed, B. D., & Armstrong, D. G. (1988). *Professional Management.* London: The Grubb Institute.

Rice, A. K. (1965). *Learning for Leadership.* London: Tavistock.

Rioch, M. (1979). The A. K. Rice group relations conferences as a reflection of society. In W. G. Lawrence (Ed.), *Exploring Individual and Organizational Boundaries.* London/New York: Wiley.

Selvini-Palazzoli, M., Boscolo, L., Cecchin, G., & Prata, G. (1978). *Paradox and Counterparadox.* New York: Jason Aronson.

Selvini-Palazzoli, M., Boscolo, L., Cecchin, G., & Prata, G. (1980). Hypothesizing–circularity–neutrality: three guidelines for the conductor of the session. *Family Process, 19* (1): 3–12.

Senge, P. M. (1990). *The Fifth Discipline: The Art and Practice of the Learning Organization.* London: Century.

Simon, F. B., Stierlin, H., & Wynne, L. C. (1985). *The Language of Family*

Therapy: A Systematic Vocabulary and Sourcebook. New York: Family Process Press.

Skynner, R. (1989). *Institutes and How to Survive Them.* London: Methuen.

Smith, K. K., & Berg, D. N. (1987). *Paradoxes of Group Life.* San Francisco/London: Jossey-Bass.

Tomm, K. (1985). Circular interviewing: a multifaceted clinical tool. In D. Cambell & R. Draper (Eds.), *Applications of the Milan Approach to Family Therapy.* London: Grune & Stratton.

Tomm, K. (1988). *Interventive Interviewing.* Unpublished conference paper.

Torbert, W. R. (1991). *The Power of Balance: Transforming Self, Society and Scientific Enquiry.* Newbury Park/London: Sage.

Torbert, W. R., & Fisher, D. (1992). Autobiographical awareness as a catalyst for managerial and organizational learning. *Management Education and Development, 23* (Part 3): 184–198.

Watzlawick, P., Bavelas, J. B., & Jackson, D. D. (1967). *The Pragmatics of Human Communication.* New York/London: W. W. Norton.

Watzlawick, P., Weakland, J., & Fisch, R. (1974). *Change: Principles of Problem Formation and Problem Resolution.* New York: W. W. Norton.

White, M., & Epston, D. (1990). *Narrative Means to Therapeutic Ends.* New York/London: W. W. Norton.

Wiener, N. (1954/1967). *The Human Use of Human Beings.* New York: Avon.

Wilden, A. (1972). *System and Structure.* London: Tavistock.

Wynne, L. C., McDaniel, S. H., & Weber, T. T. (1986). *Systems Consultation: A New Perspective for Family Therapy.* New York: Guilford.

Zohar, D. (1990). *The Quantum Self.* London: Bloomsbury.

Grubb Institute publications may be obtained from: The Grubb Institute, Cloudesley Street, London N1 0HU (071-278 8061).

INDEX